POETRY
Made Visible

POETRY
Made Visible

⌇

BOSTON SITES for Poetry
Lovers, Art Lovers & Lovers

⌇

KEN BRESLER

Poetry Made Visible

Copyright © 2017 Ken Bresler

FIRST EDITION, 2017

ISBN-13: 978-1974616275
ISBN-10:1974616274

Photography: Ken Bresler
Cover and Book Layout: Doreen Hann

Maps of the Davis Square Station: Angela Nannini of nanninidesign.com

TO THE NEXT GENERATION:

"It's so strange the way things turn."

~ Peter Gabriel, from "Don't Give Up"

Because life's too short to blush,
I keep my blood tucked in.
I won't be mortified
by what I drive or the flaccid
vivacity of my last dinner party.
I take my cue from statues posing only
in their shoulder pads of snow: all January
you can see them working on their granite tans.

~ Excerpt, "About Face" by Alice Fulton

This sculpture that stands before me; I was blinded,
I could not see. Silence is the only thing that separates us.

Within this stone does your heart beat? Do you yearn for
passion like me?

I look at the statue next to me, with the sense of compassion and knowingly, one day this stone will break and you
will love me.

~ "Statue of Love" by Sabrina A. Shields

TABLE OF CONTENTS

INTRODUCTION

This guidebook is for tourists and natives of the Boston area, for students and teachers, for lovers of poetry and lovers of public art.

You've heard of a date movie? This can be a date book. Take this book on a date. This book is for lovers and lovers-to-be.

This book has four chapters: Poetry made visible in the Boston Public Library, on the Orange Line of the MBTA/ Southwest Corridor Park, in dispersed sites throughout Boston, and in the Davis Square Station on the Red Line.

Chapter 1
Boston Public Library

Boston Public Library

I recommend that you take this tour on a sunny day. The second stop is outside and the third stop is hard to see without natural light.

Boston is the hub of the universe, as the expression goes. The heart of Boston may well be Copley Square. And a jewel of Copley Square, although not the only one, is the Boston Public Library.

It is a "palace for the people," said the architect of the original library building, Charles Follen McKim. It is a "noble treasure house of learning," said Mary Antin, a Russian immigrant, in her memoir.

I call it "The Temple of Poetry."

The Boston Public Library in Copley Square (Boston has many branch libraries in other parts of the city) consists of two attached buildings. The older building opened in 1895. Designed by Charles Follen McKim, it is sometimes called the McKim Building. The newer building opened in 1972. It was designed by Philip Johnson and is sometimes called the Johnson Building.

Enter the new building at 700 Boylston Street. Turn right into the expansive reading room for fiction, marked by an overhead "Fiction" sign. A set of two long windows faces Exeter Street.

FICTION READING ROOM

A bust of Maya Angelou sits on the bookshelves, facing the right window.

A photograph of this bust appears on the back cover, next to the spine, the second photograph from the top.

Title: *Maya Angelou*
Artist: Steve Paterson
Medium: Resin
Date: 2015

This bust of a craggy and serious-looking Maya Angelou was installed in the library when the Johnson Building's renovation was completed in 2016. Angelou (1928–2014) was a poet, but also an autobiographer, best known for *I Know Why the Caged Bird Sings*. She recited her poem "On the Pulse of Morning" at President Bill Clinton's first inauguration in 1993.

If you have a smartphone and you're interested in reading a poem by Angelou, search on poetryfoundation.org, poemhunter.com, poetryoutloud.org, and famouspoetsandpoems.com.

Title: *Edgar Allan Poe*
Artist: Bryan Moore
Medium: Bronze
Date: 2014

A bust of Edgar Allan Poe sits on the bookshelves, facing the left window.

This bust was also installed after the library and reading room were renovated. Poe is also commemorated by a statue near the Public Garden. For information about the statue and for two of his poems, see pages 112-121.

Leave the entrance of the Johnson Building and turn right. Go to where the Johnson Building and McKim

Building meet.

A photograph of some of these names appears on the front cover, at the bottom.

The older building's facade is carved with the names of luminaries in literature, art, science, religion, law, statecraft, and other fields. The carved names are weighted toward literary figures, especially English ones.

Of the 546 carved names (542 names, with four names accidentally duplicated), a fifth of them commemorate poets: 118 poets, by my count.

The facade is carved with no names from the twentieth or twenty-first centuries. The names were possibly carved in 1892, but they were definitely on the facade before the library opened in 1895. Although the Blagden Street side of the building has five blank panels, no names have been added since the original inscriptions.

Under the right-most window of the original building, in the left column of names, is carved the name of Omar Khayyam, the Persian poet. It is Khayyam who wrote the line, "A jug of wine, a loaf of bread—and thou."

Under the second window from the right, in the right column of names, is the carved name of August Wilhelm von Schlegel, the German poet.

Under the fourth window from the right, in the right column, is a group of carved names of four Roman poets: Titus Lucretius Carus, Gaius Valerius Catullus, Albius Tibullus, and Sextus Propertius.

Notice that the *u*'s are carved as *v*'s. There was no *u* in the Latin alphabet; *u*'s and *v*'s were the same letter. Even the non-Latin names on the library's facade use a *v* instead of a *u*; it's traditional in stone-cutting.

Under the sixth window from the right, in the left column of names, are the carved names of three French poets: Pierre-Jean Béranger, Alphonse de Lamartine, and Victor Hugo. In the center column is the carved name of William Makepeace Thackeray, the English poet. In the right column are the carved names of these poets: Félix Lope de Vega and Francisco de Quevedo, both Spanish; Adam Gottlob Oehlenschläger, Danish; Esaias Tegnér, Swedish; and Alexander Pushkin, Russian.

It is unknown who selected the notables to commemorate, and what criteria they used. Those involved in the selection process may have included James Russell Lowell, a poet and Harvard professor; Francis J. Child, a Harvard professor whose specialties included English poetry; and William R. Richards and Phineas Pierce, who were library trustees. Lowell's name appears on the facade among the notables.

If you have a smartphone and you're interested in reading a poem by any of the poets whose names are inscribed on the facade, you can search for them online by name or by searching poetryfoundation.org, poemhunter.com, poetry-outloud.org, and famouspoetsandpoems.com.

Under the seventh window from the right, in the left column of names, are the carved names of American poets Ralph Waldo Emerson, Nathaniel Hawthorne, Edgar Allan Poe, and Henry David Thoreau. All had Massachusetts connections. Poe is also commemorated by a bust in the library and a statue near the Public Garden. See page 112.

In the center column are the carved names of French poets François Villon, Pierre de Ronsard, and François de Malherbe. In the right column: French poets Jean de La Fontaine, Nicolas Boileau-Despréaux, and Voltaire.

Emerson, Hawthorne, and Thoreau are not known primarily for their poetry, which raises the questions: Who is a poet? And whom do I count as a poet?

George Sand, whose name appears under the previous window, said, "He who draws noble delights from the sentiments of poetry is a true poet, though he has never written a line in all his life."

That *might* be true. It's a, well, poetic definition of "poet," but not sufficient for this discussion. Joseph Story, the Supreme Court justice (whose name appears on the Dartmouth Street facade, under the third window from the left), wrote poetry, but I'm not going to consider him a poet. It's a judgment call.

Forgive me if I've made the wrong call in not listing various luminaries among poets. I'm not trying to dishonor any poet or offend any readers. And forgive me if I've missed anyone whose name is inscribed and, according to consensus, was a poet.

Here's a poem by Thoreau in its entirety. It is not an excerpt.

My life has been the poem I would have writ,
But I could not both live and utter it.

Under the eighth window from the right, in the left column, are the carved names of these poets: Thomas Chatterton, English; Robert Burns, Scottish; William Wordsworth, English; Walter Scott, Scottish; and Samuel Taylor Coleridge, English. The carved names in the center column are of these English poets: Percy Bysshe Shelley, John Keats, Thomas Hood, Alfred, Lord Tennyson, and Elizabeth Barrett Browning. The right column has the carved name of American poet Philip Freneau.

Robert Burns is commemorated by a statue in Boston's Winthrop Square. See page 162.

In some places on the facade, the reason why names were grouped is apparent. Under this window, for example, is a concentration of English poets. However, the way that names were organized is only general.

In the following poem, "certes," which rhymes with "thirties," is an archaic word for "certainly."

Sonnets From the Portuguese, Sonnet XIV
by Elizabeth Barrett Browning

If thou must love me, let it be for nought
Except for love's sake only. Do not say
'I love her for her smile—her look—her way

Of speaking gently,—for a trick of thought
That falls in well with mine, and certes brought
A sense of pleasant ease on such a day'—
For these things in themselves, Belovèd, may
Be changed, or change for thee,—and love, so wrought,
May be unwrought so. Neither love me for
Thine own dear pity's wiping my cheeks dry,—
A creature might forget to weep, who bore
Thy comfort long, and lose thy love thereby!
But love me for love's sake, that evermore
Thou may'st love on, through love's eternity.

Under the next window, the third window from the left, in the left column are the carved names of the Italian poet Francesco Petrarch, and then the English poets Geoffrey Chaucer, Edmund Spenser, George Herbert, and Samuel Butler. In the center column: English poets Henry Wotton, John Donne, Edmund Waller, and Edward Young. In the right column: English poets Alexander Pope, James Thomson, Thomas Gray, Oliver Goldsmith, and William Cowper.

Under the second window from the left, in the left column, are the carved names of German poets Wolfram von Eschenbach, Hans Sachs, Friedrich Gottlieb Klopstock, Wolfgang von Goethe, and Johann Heinrich Voss. In the center column: German poets Johann Christoph Friedrich von Schiller, Johann Ludwig Uhland, Karl Theodor Koërner, and Heinrich Heine. In the right column, these poets: George Eliot, Robert Southey, and Thomas Campbell, all English; Thomas Moore, Irish; and George Gordon (Lord) Byron, English.

She Walks in Beauty
by George Gordon (Lord) Byron

She walks in beauty, like the night
    Of cloudless climes and starry skies;
And all that's best of dark and bright
    Meet in her aspect and her eyes:
Thus mellow'd to that tender light
    Which heaven to gaudy day denies.

One shade the more, one ray the less,
    Had half impair'd the nameless grace
Which waves in every raven tress,
    Or softly lightens o'er her face;
Where thoughts serenely sweet express
    How pure, how dear their dwelling-place.

And on that cheek, and o'er that brow,
    So soft, so calm, yet eloquent,
The smiles that win, the tints that glow,
    But tell of days in goodness spent,
A mind at peace with all below,
    A heart whose love is innocent!

Under the first window from the left, in the center column, are the carved names of five American poets: William Cullen Bryant, Henry Wadsworth Longfellow, John Greenleaf Whittier, Oliver Wendell Holmes, Sr. (not the Supreme Court justice, but his father), and James Russell Lowell. They were all Massachusetts poets, or at least had Massachusetts roots. Longfellow is commemorated with a bridge. See page 77.

Turn the corner onto Dartmouth Street.

Under the first window from the right, in the left column are the carved names of Aeschylus and Sophocles, Greek poets; Terence, a poet born in Africa who wrote in Latin; Pedro Calderón de la Barca, a Spanish poet; and John Marston, an English poet. In the center column are the carved names of Miguel de Cervantes, the Spanish poet; Vittorio Alfieri, the Italian poet; and James Shirley and William Congreve, English poets. In the right column: the immortal William Shakespeare and his fellow English poets John Dryden, Christopher Marlowe, and Ben Jonson; Irish poet Richard Brinsley Sheridan; and English poet Philip Massinger.

Under the third window from the right, in the left column, is the carved name of Walter Raleigh, the English poet.

Under the fourth window from the right, in the left column is the carved name of the English poet Joseph Addison. In the center column: English poets Philip Sidney and Izaak Walton. In the right column: English poets Matthew Arnold, George Chapman, and Edward Fairfax; and the French poet Jean-Baptiste Racine.

Under the fifth window from the right, in the left column are the carved names of the Greek poets Homer, Sappho, Anacreon, Simonides of Ceos, Hesiod, Theocritus, and Titus Maccius Plautus. In the center column are the names of the Roman poets Horace, Publius Ovidius Naso (Ovid), and Juvenal. In the right column: Italian poets Dante Alghieri, Torquato Tasso, Pietro Bonaventura Metastasio, and Giacomo Leopardi; Firdusi, the Persian poet; Luis de Camoens, the Portuguese poet; and Alessandro Manzoni, the Italian poet.

Under this window are the names of 17 poets, more than under any other window. I call it "the Poets' Window."

Walk past the entrance on Dartmouth Street to the other end of the facade.

Under the second window from the left, in the left column, are the carved names of Pindar, the Greek poet; and Publius Vergilius Maro (Virgil) and Marcus Annaeus Lucanus (Lucan), both Roman poets.

Turn the corner onto Blagden Street.

Under the second window from the right, in the left column, is the carved name of Jean Froissart, the French poet.

Under the fourth window from the right, in the right column, are the carved names of Kālidāsa, the Sanskrit poet, who may have lived near the Himalayas; Ludovico Ariosto, the Italian poet; and these English poets: Robert Herrick, John Milton, and Abraham Cowley.

Return to Dartmouth Street. Go to the original entrance of the Boston Public Library facing Copley Square. Enter the set of doors leading from the outside to the Vestibule, which is a relatively small and simple lobby. In front of you is a second set of doors.

DOORS

These six bronze doors, by Daniel Chester French, the American master, each depict a personification of an art or virtue. The second door from the left is Poetry. Look at the top of this tall door—10 feet, 8 inches high—for the medallion reading "Poetry."

Poetry wears a classical robe and a halo. She holds a lit lamp with a double nozzle. A small figure serves as the knob on the lid of the lamp. Smoke rises from the flames in curlicues. Three stars either emanate from the smoke or represent the night sky.

Under the figure of Poetry, a legend (inscription) appears in all capital letters. You may have to kneel to read it: "True poetry is like the loadstone which both attracts the needle and supplies it with magnetic power." The source of this legend, and whether the sculptor selected it, is unknown.

Title: *Doors, Boston Public Library*
Artist: Daniel Chester French
Medium: Bronze
Date: 1894–1902

Loadstone, also spelled "lodestone," is a naturally magnetized form of the mineral magnetite. The legend about poetry is surprisingly unpoetic. But it is prescient, too. You can consider it an anticipation of magnetic poetry that was prevalent in the last decades of the twentieth century: words on magnets that people arranged on refrigerators and file cabinets to compose poetry.

Of the five other legends, one is derived from poetry. The legend under Music, which is to the left of Poetry, is an excerpt from "Arcades," a masque (a performance piece) by the poet John Milton:

> Such sweet compulsion doth in music lie,
> To lull the daughters of Necessity,
> And keep unsteady Nature to her law.

From left to right, the doors portray Music, Poetry, Knowledge, Wisdom, Truth, and Romance.

Doors
by Carl Sandburg

> An open door says, "Come in."
> A shut door says, "Who are you?"
> Shadows and ghosts go through shut doors.
> If a door is shut and you want it shut,
> why open it?
> If a door is open and you want it open,
> why shut it?
> Doors forget but only doors know what it is
> doors forget.

Pass through the bronze doors and face the Main Staircase.

MAIN ENTRANCE HALL

Overhead in the elegant lobby called the Main Entrance Hall are nine vaulted domes. Three rows of vaulted domes run from the Vestibule behind you to the Main Staircase in front of you. Each row has three vaulted domes. Each vaulted dome has names fashioned in mosaic.

Mosaic
by Joyce Chelmo

Amidst the dull maize sunset
and the chill of soon to come night.
I wait for darkness to descend, a welcome friend.
My muse rises from depths, a whisper
barely audible, pressing, a hunger
that needs to be fed.

She sings of present and past alike.
Memories that have to be told,
Thoughts of youth, things of now, shards
of my life gathered, abstract pictures
painted in mosaics of me.

Three poets' names appear in this hall, all in the center row. As you enter, the first dome commemorates Nathaniel Hawthorne on the left. The third dome, which is toward the stairs, commemorates Henry Wadsworth Longfellow on the left, and Ralph Waldo Emerson on the right.

Some names in the Main Entrance Hall also appear on the library's facade. As with the facade's inscriptions, it is unknown who selected these names. They are all Americans.

Go up the stairs. When they branch, turn left. Pass the lion, and stop halfway up the rest of the stairs.

MURALS ON THE MAIN STAIRCASE

On the Main Staircase are eight murals representing poetry, philosophy, and science. Across from you, above the opposite staircase, are the three murals about poetry. They were painted by Pierre Puvis de Chavannes.

In 1895, Herbert Small wrote in the *Handbook of the New Public Library in Boston*:

> Title: *Pastoral Poetry*
> Title: *Dramatic Poetry*
> Title: *Epic Poetry*
> Artist: Pierre Puvis de Chavannes
> Medium: Paint on canvas
> Date: 1896

Pastoral Poetry is summed up in the figure of Virgil, as the author of the famous Eclogues which for eighteen centuries have been the best known models of conventional rural verse. He stands in front of a clump of slender trees, contemplating nature in a landscape of idyllic beauty, wooded, hilly, and well watered. On a bank in the distance, two shepherds—for such they may be taken to be in view of the subject of the panel—are idling away the summer's afternoon.

In *Dramatic Poetry* Æschylus is to be seen sitting upon the edge of a cliff overlooking the sea, meditating his tragedy of *Prometheus Bound*. At a little distance a steep rock rises sharply from the water; on this the artist has visualized a scene of the play—Prometheus, condemned by the gods to ages of punishment for stealing fire from heaven and giving it into the possession of man, lies shackled upon the rock, naked and exposed to the attack of the undying vulture which feeds perpetually upon his vitals. The Oceanides rise from the water, and, floating around him in the air, endeavor to soothe his pain by their song.

The last panel—*Epic Poetry*—shows the blind Homer, seated up on a great stone by the roadside. He is represented as the wandering minstrel, or rhapsodist of the heroic age, with staff and lyre, the latter now laid beside him on the ground. The deep revery into which he has fallen is interrupted by the appearance of two female figures, of noble mien and carriage, personifying his two great poems, the *Iliad* and *Odyssey*. The former wears a helmet and carries a spear, in token of the continual warfare in which she lives; while the *Odyssey* has an oar for her voyages and adventures by sea.

The names of Virgil, Æschylus and Homer also appear on the library's facade.

Continue up the Main Staircase.

PUVIS DE CHAVANNES LOGGIA

Puvis de Chavannes also painted the mural at the top of the Main Staircase. This area is called the Puvis de Chavannes Loggia or the Puvis de Chavannes Vestibule.

Title: *Les Muses Inspiratrices Acclament Le Génie, Messager de Lumière / The Muses of Inspiration Welcoming Genius, Spirit of Light*
Artist: Pierre Puvis de Chavannes
Medium: Paint on canvas
Date: 1896

This mural, *Les Muses Inspiratrices Acclament Le Génie, Messager de Lumière/ The Muses of Inspiration Welcoming Genius, Spirit of Light*, depicts the nine muses, who were sisters. Among the muses are Calliope, the muse of epic poetry; Erata, the muse of love poetry; and Euterpe, the muse of elegiac poetry (and song). The other muses are Clio, history; Melpomene, tragedy; Polyhymnia, hymns; Terpsichore, dance; Thalia, comedy; and Urania, astronomy.

The Greek poet Sappho (who was born between 630 and 612 B.C.E., and died around 570 B.C.E.) wrote that the Muses "granted me honor/by the gift of their works."

In addition to Sappho, other poets, including Emily Dickinson and William Blake, have written poems about the muses. One such poem is on page 27.

In this mural, it is unclear which muse is which. Some depictions of the muses distinguish them by the objects they hold. For instance, Calliope often holds a writing tablet; Erata often, a cithara, a musical instrument like a lyre; and Euterpe, an aulos, a musical instrument like a flute. However, none of the muses in this mural holds a writing tablet or flute-like instrument, and six hold lyre-like instruments. Puvis de Chavannes may not have intended to distinguish the muses.

In the center is Apollo. On the left side of the doorway, the seated figure is Study. On the right side of the doorway, the seated figure is Contemplation.

Enter the door between Study and Contemplation.

BATES HALL

Bates Hall is named for Joshua Bates, the library's original benefactor. The hall's frieze, the band around the top of the walls, contains 34 names.

Directly above this entrance is Homer's name. Clockwise, with other names interspersed, are the names of these poets: Milton, Dante, Goethe, Shakespeare, and Cervantes. All six poets' names also appear on the library's facade. As with the names on the facade and in the Main Entrance Hall, it is unknown who selected them. Among the 34 names in the frieze is "Buonarroti"—for Michelangelo di Lodovico Buonarroti Simoni, whom Americans generally know as Michelangelo.

Sonnet 116
by William Shakespeare
Let me not to the marriage of true minds
Admit impediments. Love is not love
Which alters when it alteration finds,

Or bends with the remover to remove.
O no, it is an ever fixèd mark
That looks on tempests and is never shaken;
It is the star to every wand'ring barque,
Whose worth's unknown, although his height be taken.
Love's not time's fool, though rosy lips and cheeks
Within his bending sickle's compass come;
Love alters not with his brief hours and weeks,
But bears it out even to the edge of doom.
  If this be error and upon me proved,
  I never writ, nor no man ever loved.

Shakespeare is also commemorated by a bust in Chinatown. For information about the bust and two other Shakespeare sonnets, see pages 159-161.

Bates Hall contains busts of several poets. *Face the door that you entered. The second bust* is that of Sir Walter Scott. (That's the location at the time of this writing. The location of busts may change.) He wears a tartan garment (the pattern is carved into the marble) and a brooch to clasp it.

Title: Walter Scott bust
Artist: John R. S. A. Hutchinson's copy of Sir Francis Chantrey's bust
Medium: Marble
Date: 1896–1899

Title: Thomas Gold Appleton bust
Artist: Nicola Cantalamessa-Papotti
Medium: White marble
Date: 1873

Title: Oliver Wendell Holmes bust
Artist: Richard Edwin Brooks
Medium: Bronze on black wooden pedestal
Date: 1896

Title: Henry Wadsworth Longfellow bust
Artist: Samuel James Kitson
Medium: Marble on pedestal of verde antique marble
Date: 1879

The third bust to the right is that of Thomas Gold Appleton. His bust faces, on the opposite wall, that of Oliver Wendell Holmes. Holmes wrote a poem for the library's dedication in 1888 that includes this line: "This palace is the people's own!"

Face the entrance again. The second bust is Henry Wadsworth Longfellow. His beard flows and he looks off beyond your left shoulder. Longfellow is also commemorated by a bridge. For information about it and for two of his poems, see pages 77-82.

The library also owns busts of John Greenleaf Whittier and of Cervantes. At the time of this writing, they are not on public display.

The names of Scott, Appleton, Holmes, Longfellow, Whittier, and Cervantes are also carved on the facade.

This poem is set in Bates Hall.

In the main reading room
by Deborah Leipziger

I
I am not sure why you brought me here
Except to share what you love with me
There is real intimacy in silence

My earring falls to the marble floor
And the sound echoes
Mother of pearl

II

I watch you circumnavigate the room
Paying homage to the books and sculptures

Do you know that I am watching you?
Can you feel my gaze?

III

Your hand lingers on my back
as if there are notes to be played

the pod from the tree curves
so full of seeds

what music are you tapping on my back, I long to ask.

Deborah Leipziger is a poet, author, and professor of corporate responsibility. She teaches at the Simmons School of Management and other places, and lives in Brookline. She is co-founder of the online journal *Soul-Lit*. Her book of poetry is *Flower Map*.

Leave Bates Hall through the door you entered. In the Puvis de Chavannes Loggia, turn right, then turn right again, and go up the stairs.

At the top of the stairs, go straight and enter the Wiggin Gallery. Turn right through a doorway made of rose-colored stone. (You'll be walking around the courtyard, which is outside.) Pass the printing presses on the left. Walk under the exit sign. Turn right and enter the Arts Department.

On the right, on the wall punctuated by windows overlooking the courtyard, are various sculptures. The second one is a bust of John Boyle O'Reilly, the Irish poet. He wears a moustache and looks eminent and poised. Notice the artist's name and the date of completion on the right side.

Title: John Boyle O'Reilly bust
Artist: John Talbott Donoghue
Medium: Bronze
Date: 1897

A Disappointment
by John Boyle O'Reilly

Her hair was a waving bronze, and her eyes
   Deep wells that might cover a brooding soul;
And who, till he weighed it, could ever surmise
   That her heart was a cinder instead of a coal!

O'Reilly is also commemorated by a statue and bas-relief silhouette in Boston. For information about the statue and for two other O'Reilly poems, see pages 82–86. For information about the bas-relief, see page 169.

After O'Reilly is Julia Ward Howe, who lived in South Boston. She wears a toga-like robe and a subtle tiara. She is best known for writ-

Title: Julia Ward Howe bust
Artist: Shobal Vail Clevenger
Medium: Marble
Date: 1839–40

ing the lyric to "Battle-Hymn of the Republic." (She included a hyphen in the title, as was the style.) She wrote it for an existing Union song with a chorus of "Glory, glory, hal-lelujah." In other words, Howe wrote the stanzas but not the chorus or music. That's why "Glory, glory, hallelujah" doesn't appear below.

Battle-Hymn of the Republic
By Julia Ward Howe

Mine eyes have seen the glory of the coming of the Lord:
He is trampling out the vintage where the grapes of wrath are stored;
He hath loosed the fateful lightning of his terrible swift sword:
 His truth is marching on.

I have seen Him in the watch-fires of a hundred circling camps;
They have builded Him an altar in the evening dews and damps;
I can read His righteous sentence by the dim and flaring lamps.
 His Day is marching on.

I have read a fiery gospel, writ in burnished rows of steel:
"As ye deal with my contemners, so with you my grace shall deal;
Let the Hero, born of woman, crush the serpent with his heel,
 Since God is marching on."

He has sounded forth the trumpet that shall never call retreat;
He is sifting out the hearts of men before his judgment-seat:
Oh! be swift, my soul, to answer Him! be jubilant, my feet!
 Our God is marching on.

In the beauty of the lilies Christ was born across the sea,
With a glory in his bosom that transfigures you and me:
As he died to make men holy, let us die to make men free,
 While God is marching on.

Retrace your steps.

As you leave the Boston Public Library, read these excerpts from poems:

> America why are your libraries full of tears?
> ~ Excerpt, "America" by Allen Ginsberg

> How I got from then to now
> is the mystery that could fill a whole library
> much less an arbitrary stanza
> ~ Excerpt, "Birthday Poem" by Al Young

> Shut not your doors to me proud libraries,
> For that which was lacking on all your well-fill'd shelves, yet
>   needed most, I bring.
> ~ Excerpt, "Shut Not Your Doors" by Walt Whitman

> Not marble nor the gilded monuments
> Of princes shall outlive this powerful rhyme....
> ~ Excerpt, Sonnet 55 by William Shakespeare.

Questions

Do you agree with Shakespeare? Are there gilded monuments that have outlived powerful rhymes? Are there rhymes that have outlived monuments?

Whitman wrote, "Shut not your doors to me proud libraries,/For that which was lacking on all your well-fill'd shelves, yet needed most, I bring." What do you bring to a library?

If you could add names to the blank panels on the Blagden Street facade of the Boston Public Library, which poets would you add? Which non-poets?

Do you agree with George Sand, who said, "He who draws noble delights from the sentiments of poetry is a true poet, though he has never written a line in all his life"? George Sand was the pen name of a woman, Amantine-Lucile-Aurore Dupin (1804-1876), a French writer, who surely meant to include women in her statement.

Have the Muses ever visited you and inspired you? Is there a person who is your Muse?

Of the nine Muses, one each is for epic poetry, love poetry, elegiac poetry (and song), history, tragedy, hymns, dance, comedy, and astronomy. What other fields should have Muses? Architecture? Computer coding?

John Boyle O'Reilly wrote a poem about expecting a person to have certain traits based on the person's appearance and being surprised that the expectation was not true. Has that happened to you?

We think of a hymn as religious. Is the title "The Battle-Hymn of the Republic" incongruous? Did you know that it had more than one stanza?

The Boston Public Library has been called a "palace for the people," a "noble treasure house of learning," and "The Temple of Poetry." What would you call it?

Can you write a poem about the Boston Public Library or your favorite library?

CHAPTER 2
The Orange Line/ Southwest Corridor Park

The Orange Line/
Southwest Corridor
Park

Installations of poetry—poems carved in stone—had their origin in a highway.

A controversial highway project, the Southwest Corridor or Southwest Expressway, was finally killed in 1973. Eight lanes of traffic had been planned to link Route 95, southwest of Boston, and a proposed Inner Belt Expressway (which also was never built) in Boston.

After the Southwest Corridor was halted, a wide barren swath ran through Boston neighborhoods. Decades later, it is un-

Protest graffiti against the Southwest Corridor. PHOTOGRAPHER UNKNOWN

clear—because documents are not freely available and memories have faded—how far the project progressed; how many buildings, homes, and businesses were demolished; and how much of the swath was due to a railroad right of way as opposed to bulldozing and other demolition. Almost 2,000 housing units and several hundred businesses may have been lost.

In any case, it took years, but the swath of unused land was given a new purpose, or purposes, actually. The Orange Line of the Massachusetts Bay Transportation Authority (MBTA), which was an elevated line for the portion it ran above ground, was shifted to the Southwest Corridor. New stations were built and the elevated line was torn down. This new part of the Orange Line opened in 1987. (This might have happened even if the Southwest Corridor Expressway had been built. According to at least one source, the new part of the Orange Line was going to run on the highway's median.) And a linear park opened two years later, the Southwest Corridor Park, with paths for cycling, running, and walking.

The two purposes, the Orange Line and the park, are in turn linked by a literary project. The park contains installations of poetry and prose carved into stone. Nine installations, one at each of nine Orange Line stations, have a poem and a short story or other prose piece.

"There was a lot of hurt in the neighborhoods and this was an opportunity to leave a legacy where the scars had been," said Pamela Worden. Worden is the former president and CEO of the nonprofit group Urban Arts, Inc., which was instrumental in the literary project. "We wanted to use words because we are surrounded by words. We have advertising screaming at us. We felt there ought to be words in the public environment that speak to us more deeply."

Eileen Meny, who was the project director, said, "We wanted the writing to reflect a sense of place for each neighborhood. The idea was that when riders left a subway station, the poems and short stories would reflect the character and people of that community."

The poetry and prose pieces were chosen in a blind competition—resulting in the selection of both well-known and unknown poets and writers. Because this book is about poetry, it focuses on the poems.

Getting There

As noted, nine stations have literary installations. Although this chapter discusses the Forest Hills Station first and the Chinatown Station last, you can start at any station between Forest Hills and Chinatown and go in either direction.

For directions to the stations, see mbta.com. If you're visiting more than one station at a time, you want to do so as inexpensively and conveniently as possible. So also check mbta.com for information about fares and passes.

You can also visit the poetry installations by bicycle or on foot. The Orange Line and the Southwest Corridor Park run parallel to each other for the stations between Forest Hills and Back Bay. The park ends at Back Bay Station. It is possible to visit the remaining station, Tufts New England Medical Center, by bicycle or on foot, but you can't do it by following a path through the Southwest Corridor Park.

For directions to the Southwest Corridor Park, see swcpc. org, the website of the Southwest Corridor Park Conservancy. If you're going by bicycle or on foot, you can start at any station and go in any direction.

Most of the literary installations are near the path for cyclists, runners, and walkers. If you're visiting the installations by bicycle or on foot and can't locate them, this book gives directions from the T stations.

If you're leaving a T station and the directions in this book don't orient you sufficiently, look for the path for cyclists, runners, and walkers. If you can't see the path, look for:

• the Orange Line tracks, because the tracks parallel the path, and finding the tracks will help you find the path

• a Southwest Corridor Park sign, or

• bike racks, which are often near the path.

While you're at the T stations, consider visiting the art in them too. For more information about the art, see mbta. com/about_the_mbta/art_collection/.

Why this book includes the text of most poetry installations

I urge you to read the poetry where it is installed. This book is not meant to replace your visit to each installation.

I include the text of most poems for a few reasons. One is that the lighting isn't always optimal for reading the poems. I have visited the installations and not been able to read them, even on bright days, sometimes especially on bright days. If you're having trouble reading the poems, try reading them from an angle; reading at a slant sometimes works.

Some of the poems and prose pieces are hard to read because they are carved into multi-colored and light-colored granite. It's like trying to read letters on a camouflage pattern.

I also include the text of most poems because some visitors will not be able to kneel and read the bottom lines. Some visitors won't be able to see the top lines. I had to climb on a wall to read one poem's lines.

And "carved in stone" does not mean permanent. Some of the inscriptions are not weathering well. Frankly, this book is also a record for the future.

Go and read the poems *in situ*, as the Latin phrase goes—on site. If you're alone, read them to yourself—or out loud. If you're with someone, read them to each other. Or take turns reading portions. Or announce a poetry reading. Ask passersby if they have noticed the poetry and read it to them.

FOREST HILLS STATION

Take the elevator or follow the crowds up one of the two main staircases, which are next to the escalators. As you stand under the clock, the station has three exits. Look for the exit leading to the Arboretum, Bus Route 39, Washington Street, and South Street. Go through the doors. Go straight on the walkway. Between the third and fourth lampposts on the right are two slabs of polished brown granite.

One slab announces:

> Boston Contemporary Writers
> The literary component to the Southwest Corridor art
> program involved the solicitation of original poetry
> and prose from New England writers whose work
> reflects the experience of living or working in an
> urban environment. A panel of twenty professionals,
> with assistance from neighborhood advisors, selected
> the winning works in July, 1987. They are located along
> the Southwest Corridor Parkland....

The other slab is inscribed with this poem:

The Subway Collector
by Thomas Hurley

Sometimes I think I am my hands

and they are briefcase, shoulderbag, knapsack, purse
rushing down here, thrusting their money
at the hands that take and give

sometimes I touch their fingers
accidentally, our hands fumbling the exchange
but mostly we keep back behind the coin

sometimes when I look up
eyes pierce the glass
what do they want
-- are they looking
at their reflection between us

in a second with each
what should I say
if they ask for directions
I tell them what they know

as if they counted for me
I count only the numbers, thousands

it's the coins that count

sometimes I want disasters up there
to hold them here

to inspect each one
have them hold out their nails, their palms
remove their clothes, exhibit all parts of their bodies
force their names from them like deepest secrets

then I would place the tokens in their mouths
communion for the journey

the line lengthens
how can I be polite to so many
I do my work, I admit them
into the trains where they must hold up

against the weight of other bodies
making their rapid transit

This is the only poem about public transit in this series of installations tied to public transit.

Behind you—and hidden behind a glass and metal bus shelter—are two gray stone slabs, coming together like a V and balanced on a total of three stone circles. Carved on them is an excerpt from Ethan Canin's story "Lies."

GREEN STREET STATION

Turn right out of the station. At the corner of Green and Amory Streets is a three-sided installation of black polished granite. You can see it from the station door.

The installation includes a story by Daria MonDesire, "Reflections," and a poem. The poem uses "chile pepper," which is an alternative spelling for "chili pepper."

Drift
by Mary Bonina

Tonight the streets are dead.
I give the world the cold
        shoulder,
the frozen stare. There is clean
        snow on my brow.

At LA BOTANICA AND MARKET

I feel warmer
seeing crates of limes and
          lemons at the door.
There's a family at work inside:
blood of a hot country travels
          in their veins.
On shelves there are chile
          pepper condiments.

My nose pressed against the glass
I watch a young boy juggling
Florida "Sunkist." I begin to thaw.
When he sees me, his timing
          is destroyed
and he drops them, hugs himself
          to show me
he is sorry I'm out in the storm.

This poem is set in Worcester, where Mary Bonina grew up. It features a bodega she used to walk by that sold, in addition to food, religious items. As for why she titled it "Drift," she leaves it to readers to decide.

When "Drift" was selected for this installation, Bonina, a poet and writer of fiction and memoir, had not won any prize. "It still amazes me," she said. "People don't have a monument like that until they're dead."

Bonina's book of poetry is *Clear Eye Tea*. She lives in Cambridge.

Go out of the station. Turn right. At the corner of Boylston and Lamartine Streets is a three-sided installation of beige granite.

The installation includes a short story by Rosario Morales, "The Dinner." In the following poem, the carved word is "tigres," not "tigers":

Mrs. Báez Serves Coffee On The Third Floor
by Martín Espada

It hunches
with a brittle black spine
where they poured
gasoline on the stairs
and the bannister
and burnt it.

The fire went running
down the steps,
a naked lunatic,
calling the names
of the neighbors,
cackling in the hall.

The immigrants
ate terror with their hands
and prayed to Catholic statues
as the fire company
pumped a million gallons in

and burst the roof,
as an old man
on the top floor
with no name known
to authorities
strangled on the smoke
and stopped breathing.

Some of the people left.
There's a room
on the third floor:
high-heeled shoes kicked off,
a broken dresser,
the saint's portrait
hanging where it looked on
shrugging shoulders for years,
soot, trash, burnt tile,
a perfect black light bulb
to remember everything.

And some stayed. The old men
barechested, squatting
on the milk crates to play dominoes
in the front-stoop sun;
the younger ones, the tigres,
watching the block with unemployed faces
bitter as bad liquor;
Mrs. Báez, who serves coffee
on the third floor
from tiny porcelain cups,
insisting that we stay;
the children who live

between narrow kitchens
and charred metal doors
and laugh anyway;
the skinny man, the one
just arrived from Santo Domingo,
who cannot read or write,
with no hot water
for six weeks,
telling us in the hallway
that the landlord set the fire
and everyone knows it,
the building worth more empty.

The street organizer said it;
burn the building out,
blacken an old Dominicano's lungs
and sell
so that the money-people
can renovate
and live here
where an old Dominicano died,
over the objections
of his choking spirit.

But some have stayed.
Stayed for the malicious winter,
stayed frightened
of the white man who comes
to collect rent
and borrowing from cousins
to pay it,
stayed waiting for the next fire,

and the siren,
hysterical and late.

Someone poured gasoline
on the steps outside her door,
but Mrs. Báez
still serves coffee
in porcelain cups
to strangers,
coffee the color
of a young girl's skin
in Santo Domingo.

The poem is not set in Boston. "I wrote the poem after visiting an apartment building on the Upper West Side of Manhattan in 1981 in the company of my father, Frank Espada, a documentary photographer. The building had been torched by the landlord," Martín Espada emailed me in response to my questions. "As I understand it, the poem was installed at Stony Brook because there had been a similar arson case across the street or around the corner. People apparently believed, when they read the poem, that it was about that case."

The poem was carved as he wrote it, including line breaks. As for its permanence, he wrote: "That stone will last long after I'm gone."

Espada, once a tenants' lawyer, is an English professor at the University of Massachusetts-Amherst. His many books, most of them poetry, include these poetry books: *Vivas to Those Who Have Failed* and *A Mayan Astronomer in Hell's Kitchen*.

Use the doors on the left to leave the station. Straight ahead, past four tree planters, near a light pole, is a three-sided installation with a pyramid cap. It is light brown granite. You can see it from the station door.

The installation includes a short story by Christine Palamidessi Moore, "Grandmothers." The following poem uses the words "burdock," which is a plant whose seeds are burrs, and "veturi," which probably means a bottleneck here. A different version of this poem appeared in the Summer 1980 issue of the *Virginia Quarterly Review*.

Any Good Throat
by Christopher Gilbert

July, on the basketball court,
Willie's face is far and wooden
totem, his eyes melted pools of ice
shimmering in the high stone sun –
the sockets are darkness rotting inside.
Fifteen and can't get a summer job –
because of this the traffic jams, the
high school windows cloud with phlegm.
Everyday the long poison of waiting
for this sharp need in his gut to be
a language which is spoken in your mind,
for the name in his blood to ring
louder than this killing in his heart,
staring all day out the same caged grin
because it doesn't matter,

because this tarred-over earth
and burned and raped and cheated of growth
where his friends come root like acorns
fallen from some wound up tree
is more mother than any gray voice
in the city he might hear.

So we give him a ball
and he slams the thing luminously,
so the rim swallows its circle and cries.

A music I've learned in the evenings
draws me out, whoever I am,
past the sweet sweatdown in late sun
silence up to my knees where I bend
in the backyard working up burdock roots'
grip tapped down a good half-foot
emerges in the saline welling in my mouth
and the work-song rhythm hummed in my hands
pulling the hoe back and forth and back,
working in an honest groove, and what
with the blunder some god done made
putting me here in the world to choose
what thing is weed and what is food
makes me want to say Amen
and ripen in my *Willie*-night and sing.

In the evening indigo off the road
near the reservoir a waterfall
trickles, only waist-wide, winding down
to dam behind the spill around dead sticks
in slow gurgle toward water basin

heavy and warm after a humid week.
Along the way there are hesitations
there are layers of rock rise up awkward like
molars blocking thought in mid-sentence –
their volume a venturi for a moment
that, like any good throat, intensifies things,
then thrusts the waters forward in song.

The poet Christopher Gilbert lived from 1949 to 2007. Among other accomplishments, he received his PhD in psychology from Clark University in 1986.

ROXBURY CROSSING STATION

Leave the station and turn right. Between the covered bike racks and the bus shelter is a brown stone pillar with four sides and a pyramid cap. Carved on it is the station's prose piece, an essay by Luix Virgil Overbea, "Hometown," comparing the old and new Orange Lines. To get to the poem installation, follow the brickwork in the sidewalk on Columbus Avenue away from the corner. It will lead you toward, and you will see, a slab of gray granite with a slanted face. This is the poem:

At Roxbury Crossing
by Jeanette DeLello Winthrop

I leave the candy store and walk past
the grocery store I never enter;
come to the railroad bridge;

heavy granite pilings streaked with droppings,
black steel beams. The joinings
create inky caves where pigeons roost.
With rustling of wings, the world changes.
Under there it never snows.
Sound recedes; only cooing overhead.
In such caves in the Galapagos, bats live.
I rush through, holding my breath.
I breathe again at the red brick
police station flying the American flag.
Safely around the corner, the mingled smell
of fresh cut leather and glue comes
from the open door of the cobbler.
From where I stand I can see
the round, shiny nail heads on the
unevenly worn floorboards, the shelves
of shoes tied together in pairs.
There's a built in bench under the
front window. My father likes to sit here
in the evening talking to his friends,
reliving life on the Adriatic.
I wonder if he ever told them
my favorite story, how he, the
farm boy cleaned his teeth in
the morning by eating watermelon
freshly sliced in the early sun.

This poem is Winthrop's first published work—and it was published in granite.

The corner of Columbus Avenue and Tremont Street has a historical installation depicting what the Southwest Corridor Expressway would have looked like if it had been built; a map of the planned project; a photograph of protest graffiti against the project, which appears on page 43; and a timeline, including the park's dedication in 1989. Across Tremont Street at the bus shelter on the bridge over the Orange Line are photographs of old Roxbury and the old Orange Line.

RUGGLES STATION

Follow the crowds and leave the station. There is one set of gates. Use the leftmost one or the one next to it. Ahead is a two-sided gray granite slab, looking like a large gravestone.

This is the only poetry installation inside a station. The poem's reference to "six troubles" is from Job 5:19. Patter-rollers were night watchmen hired to patrol plantations. The word appears in many slave narratives.

Canebrake is a cane thicket. "Ahma" is possibly short for "I'm going to." It is appropriate that this poem spells "desperate" as "despirit," as in "dispirited" or "de-spirited." The poem is carved on both sides of the slab.

Harriet Tubman
aka Moses
by Samuel Allen

High in the darkening heavens
the wind swift, the storm massing

the giant arrow rose, a crackling arch, a sign
        above the fleeing band of people,
toy figures in the canebrake
        far below.

In the distance, moving up quickly
came the patterrollers
bloodhounds loping, silent.

Minutes before, one of the fleeing band had fallen
the others for a moment waited
but he did not rise.
A small dark woman stood above him.
His words were slow to come and more a groan:

        Can't make it, just can't make it
        You all go head without me.

Moses pulled out her revolver and she quietly said:

        Move or die.

        You ain't stoppin now
        You *can't* stop now
        You gonna move
        Move or die.

        If you won't go on
        Gonna risk us all
        Ahma send your soul to glory, I said move!

Long time now, I got it figgered out
Ev'ry child a God got a double right, death
or liberty, Move, now
or you will die.

Listen to me

Way back yonder
            down in bondage
                        on my knee
Th' moment that He gave his promise -
I was free

                        (Walk, children!)

He said that when destruction rages
He is a rock -
            the Rock of Ages

Declared that when the tempest ride
He just come mosey
            straight -
            to my side.

                        (Don't you get weary!)
Promised me the despirit hour
be the signal for His power
Hounddogs closin on the track

            Sunlight

and a thunderclap!

        (How you get weary?)

Bloodhound quickenin on the scent
Over my head, yesss

       the heavens rent!

O He's a father he is a mother
A sister He will

       be your brother
Supplies the harvest, He raises up the grain
O don't you feel – it's fallin now

       the blessed rain.

Don't make no diffunce if you weary
Don't mean a hoot owl if you scaird
He was with us in the six troubles
He won't desert you in the seventh.

Get on up now

That's it, no need a gettin weary
There is a glory there!

There be a great rejoicin

       no more sorrow

       shout'n *newuh* tire

       a great camp meetin

         in that land.

By fire in heaven she was guided
saved by stream
    and by water reed
By her terrible grimace of faith
    beautiful and defiant,
Till, for a moment
    in the long journey
    came the first faint glimpse
    of the stars   the everlasting stars   shining clear
    over the free
        cold
            land.

Samuel Washington Allen (1917–2015) was a poet, and among other things, a Harvard-educated lawyer.

To get to the prose installation, "Four Letters from Home," face the gates to the station. Turn left. Follow the covered walkway to its end. You'll pass three large two-sided panels depicting the history of Roxbury in the eighteenth, nineteenth, and twentieth centuries. As you leave the station, four gray stone slabs are on the right. They are near the Northeastern University International Village, facing the bike racks, along a path of the Southwest Corridor Park. The four letters are fictional descriptions of Roxbury from residents to their families whom they have left: a letter to Maine in 1834, to Ireland in 1886, to Poland in 1929, and to Georgia (the southern American state) in 1960.

MASSACHUSETTS
AVENUE STATION

You can cross Massachusetts Avenue (which Bostnians call "Mass Ave") to the poem installation or use an underpass.

If you use the underpass, exit the gates, but don't go up the stairs. To the left of the stairs going up is an unmarked staircase going down. Go down these stairs. Walk through the underpass and go up one set of stairs. Bear left and go through the doors leading outside. (Do not take the short second set of stairs up to Mass Ave.) Right outside the door, on the right, is what looks like a round coffee table made out of black granite.

If you cross Mass Ave, exit the gates and go up the stairs to the street. Cross the street. Pass under the gray metal structure. Go down a short set of stairs. On the left is what looks like a round coffee table made out of black stone.

The installation may be intended to resemble a bass drum on its side. It is the only installation whose words are on a horizontal surface. In the winter, snow can obscure it. If it has rained, it may be hard to read.

Drum
by Sharon Cox (Howell)

Let your head be your drum
  Let your heart be the strings
    And your whole body the winds
     Listen to the music of your mind
      Find serenity in the total sound
       Make no room for the melodies of
        those who never could carry a tune
         Or hear the sounds of love Hope you have
          the words of your heart turn your song
        to gold And music the music of
      a world at peace.

To read the short story by Peter Rouman, "I Know My Robe Gonna Fit Me Well," go up the stairs, walk through the gray metal structure, and cross Mass Ave. To the left is the Southwest Corridor Park. After the path bends to the left are three gray stone slabs.

BACK BAY STATION

The station has two exits. Follow the crowds toward the major exit.

Once you're moving toward the major exit, you have two options to get to the installation: Cross the street outside, or cross under the street using an underpass. For the first option, you can use the stairs, escalator, or elevator. The second option entails only stairs.

To use the underpass, go to the end of the platform. See the sign reading "Exit Here" and continue. Go through the gates. See the sign reading "Underpass to Copley Place" and continue. Take the underpass. Go up the stairs. Take the revolving door to the left and go outside. (Don't enter the mall.) You'll be facing the installation: two gray stone pillars, a black pillar behind them, and a brown stone pillar to the left.

If you're not using the underpass and are crossing Dartmouth Street: Go up the stairs, escalator, or elevator. You will have the choice of two exits to the street, separated by a large expanse of windows. Take the left exit. The left exit will take you to a cross walk. Cross the street, which is Dartmouth Street. When you get to the other side, you'll see the installation: a brown stone pillar in front of one black and two gray stone pillars.

The installation consists of four pillars. The gray and black pillars have four sides; the brown pillar, three.

The poem is on one side of the shorter gray pillar. The short story by Jane Barnes, "Counterpoint," is on all four sides of the taller gray pillar. The black pillar is blank, the only blank one in the entire nine-station project.

I did not secure permission to print Ruth Whitman's poem "If My Boundary Stops Here." It is also called "Where Is the West." However, it appears online on many sites, including on books.google.com.

Whitman (1922–99) was a poet, translator (her languages included Yiddish), and professor at Harvard University and the Massachusetts Institute of Technology.

The brown pillar repeats the information that appears outside the Forest Hills Station: background about the Boston Contemporary Writers project; the list of stations and the poems and prose pieces that are installed there; and this:

MASSACHUSETTS BAY TRANSPORTATION AUTHORITY

Michael S. Dukakis, Governor
Frederick P. Salvucci, Secretary of Transportation
Thomas P. Glynn, General Manager
Peter F. McNulty, Director of Construction
Charles H. Steward, Assistant Director of Construction
Peter C. Calcateria, Project Manager - Design
George H. Smith, Project Manager - Construction
Daniel L. Ocasio - Installation Design Consultant

URBAN ARTS, INC.

Pamela Worden, President and Chief Executive Officer
Sam Cornish, Project Coordinator
Eileen Meny, Project Director, Arts in Transit

Funded by the U.S. Department of Transportation, Urban Mass Transportation Administration as part of ARTS IN TRANSIT - THE SOUTHWEST CORRIDOR, a comprehensive public arts program managed by

Urban Arts, Inc., for the MBTA.

The fact that both the Forest Hills and Back Bay Stations have the same information about the writing project indicates that they are the project's anchors. However, the project extends one more station beyond the Back Bay Station and ends.

TUFTS NEW ENGLAND MEDICAL CENTER STATION

The station has two exits. The poem is outside one exit; the short story is inside the other exit.

For the poem, follow the signs on the platform to Tremont Street and the Wang YMCA. Pass through the gates. Go up the stairs. At the top of the stairs, turn left and take a U-turn behind the station. At the corner of Oak Street West and Tremont Street, kitty-corner from the Mass Pike Towers, is a gray carved stone.

Mr. Yee Is In The Garden
by Marea Gordett

Mr. Yee is in the garden talking to his flowers.
I don't know what he says
but I know they love him, little boats
coming to anchor in his hands.

He weeds and laughs. The thin notes
of the song glide across the soil, dark
as the Chinese fishing village
he hasn't seen in thirty years.

And beyond the garment buildings, in the next town,
Dusk slides into its car and speeds
through the red light by the depot
and arrives in its pale coat.

Sails gather in the gray:
orange tiger lilies,
roses and the fragile
pink bleeding hearts.

Mr. Yee is singing them to sleep.
On the roof the sun balances on its back.
He stands watchful, hands on his hips.
Anything could snatch them.

The poem is set on Pemberton Street in Cambridge, Gordett told me. She and her husband lived on the second floor of a three-decker. Mr. Yee was the landlord and first-floor resident. Part of his demeanor was due to his growing dementia. The reference to "the garment buildings, in the next town" is to Boston's Chinatown, the location of this installation.

Gordett is a poet, writer, and teacher of creative non-fiction in the Albany area. She was a professor of English at Tufts University from 1984 to 1992.

To read the short story, you can get to the station's other exit in two ways. If you have a T pass, return to the station and go to the opposite exit. After the gates but before the stairs, the short story is mounted on the left wall.

Or, while standing at the poem, turn left on Oak Street West. At the corner, turn left on Washington Street. Continue on Washington Street. The station is ahead of you. Turn left into the station. Go down the stairs. Before the gates, the short story is mounted on the right wall.

I recommend the short story "The Great World Transformed" by Gish Jen. It's my favorite prose piece in the project. (I like the excerpt from Ethan Canin's short story at the Forest Hills Station—but I like his entire short story better. You can read it in *Emperor of the Air.*)

Closing Quotations

Paul Simon wrote a song called "A Poem on the Underground"—but it is about a man who scrawls obscene graffiti in a subway station. It includes this verse:

> Now from his pocket he quickly flashes
> The crayon on the wall he slashes
> Deep upon the advertising
> A single-worded poem comprised of four letters.

The idea of underground poetry apparently interested Simon, because in the song "Sounds of Silence," he wrote, "The words of the prophets are written on the subway walls...."

Questions

Do you have a favorite poem or prose piece among the installations?

Did you notice...

The poems at Forest Hills, Green Street, and Stony Brook Stations, which are consecutive stations, are connected by the word "shoulder." "The Subway Collector" uses the word "shoulderbag." "Drift" uses the expression giving "the world the cold shoulder." And "Mrs. Báez Serves Coffee On The Third Floor" uses "shrugging shoulders for years."

Three poems use "blood." "Drift" includes this line: "blood of a hot country travels in their veins." "Any Good Throat" mentions "the name in his blood" ringing louder. And "Harriet Tubman aka Moses" uses "bloodhound" and "bloodhounds."

In a series of five stations, the first, middle, and last stations' poems use "blood." ("Drift" appears in the Green Street Station—two stations away from "Any Good Throat" in the Jackson Square Station. In turn, "Any Good Throat" is two stations away from "Harriet Tubman aka Moses" in the Ruggles Station.)

Three poems use yet another body part, "heart": "Any Good Throat"; "Drum," which uses it twice; and "Mr. Yee Is In The Garden," which uses "hearts."

These verbal connections among poems are probably unintentional.

Did you notice...

Three installations touch on gentrification: "I Know My Robe Gonna Fit Me Well" at the Massachusetts Avenue Station; "Mrs. Báez Serves Coffee On The Third Floor" by Martín Espada at the Stony Brook Station; and "Hometown" by Luix Virgil Overbea at the Roxbury Crossing Station.

CHAPTER 3
Dispersed Sites

Dispersed Sites

Boston has several dispersed sites related to poets—and one bridge honoring a poet. Although Boston has a number of trails, the most famous being the Freedom Trail, I'm not going to propose something like the Poets' Trail. You can visit these sites on the same day or individually, such as when you happen to be near one.

If you want to visit the dispersed sites on the same day, I recommend doing so in the order that they appear in this book. Of the eight dispersed sites in this book, five are fairly close to each other: the *Kahlil Gibran Memorial*, the Phillis Wheatley statue, the September 11 memorial, the Edgar Allan Poe statue, and the sculpture called *The Massachusetts Artifact*.

The Massachusetts Artifact is the only interior site. It is inside a state government building that is open only during business hours. So you can't visit it in the evening or on weekends or holidays.

If you want to skip the sites that are not significant sculpturally, that is, as public art, they are the *Kahlil Gibran Memorial*, the September 11 memorial, and the Shakespeare bust.

LONGFELLOW BRIDGE

Location: Intersection of Charles and Cambridge Streets.

If you're taking the T: The closest T station is Charles/ MGH on the Red Line.

If you're driving: Park on Charles or Cambridge Streets.

When the Longfellow Bridge opened in 1907, connecting Boston and Cambridge, it was called the Cambridge Bridge. It was renamed the Longfellow Bridge in 1927 to honor Henry Wadsworth Longfellow, the famous poet who lived in Cambridge and had written this poem about the predecessor bridge.

Walk onto the bridge and read or recite the next two poems.

The Bridge
By Henry Wadsworth Longfellow

I stood on the bridge at midnight,
  As the clocks were striking the hour,
And the moon rose o'er the city,
  Behind the dark church-tower.

I saw her bright reflection
  In the waters under me,
Like a golden goblet falling
  And sinking into the sea.

And far in the hazy distance
  Of that lovely night in June,
The blaze of the flaming furnace
  Gleamed redder than the moon.

Among the long, black rafters
  The wavering shadows lay,
And the current that came from the ocean
  Seemed to lift and bear them away;

As, sweeping and eddying through them,
  Rose the belated tide,
And, streaming into the moonlight,
  The seaweed floated wide.

And like those waters rushing
  Among the wooden piers,
A flood of thoughts came o'er me
  That filled my eyes with tears.

How often, oh how often,
  In the days that had gone by,
I had stood on that bridge at midnight
  And gazed on that wave and sky!

How often, oh how often,
  I had wished that the ebbing tide
Would bear me away on its bosom
  O'er the ocean wild and wide!

For my heart was hot and restless,
  And my life was full of care,
And the burden laid upon me
  Seemed greater than I could bear.

But now it has fallen from me,
  It is buried in the sea;
And only the sorrow of others
  Throws its shadow over me.

Yet whenever I cross the river
   On its bridge with wooden piers,
Like the odor of brine from the ocean
   Comes the thought of other years.

And I think how many thousands
   Of care-encumbered men,
Each bearing his burden of sorrow,
   Have crossed the bridge since then.

I see the long procession
   Still passing to and fro,
The young heart hot and restless,
   And the old subdued and slow!

And forever and forever,
   As long as the river flows,
As long as the heart has passions,
   As long as life has woes;

The moon and its broken reflection
   And its shadows shall appear,
As the symbol of love in heaven,
   And its wavering image here.

Longfellow also wrote this poem about the Charles River, which his bridge spans.

To the River Charles
by Henry Wadsworth Longfellow

River! that in silence windest
  Through the meadows, bright and free,
Till at length thy rest thou findest
  In the bosom of the sea!

Four long years of mingled feeling,
  Half in rest, and half in strife,
I have seen thy waters stealing
Onward, like the stream of life.

Thou hast taught me, Silent River!
  Many a lesson, deep and long;
Thou hast been a generous giver;
I can give thee but a song.

Oft in sadness and in illness,
  I have watched thy current glide,
Till the beauty of its stillness
  Overflowed me, like a tide.

And in better hours and brighter,
  When I saw thy waters gleam,
I have felt my heart beat lighter,
And leap onward with thy stream.

Not for this alone I love thee,
  Nor because thy waves of blue
From celestial seas above thee
  Take their own celestial hue.

Where yon shadowy woodlands hide thee,
   And thy waters disappear,
Friends I love have dwelt beside thee,
   And have made thy margin dear.

More than this; – thy name reminds me
   Of three friends, all true and tried;
And that name, like magic, binds me
   Closer, closer to thy side.

Friends my soul with joy remembers!
   How like quivering flames they start,
When I fan the living embers
   On the hearth-stone of my heart!

'T is for this, thou Silent River!
   That my spirit leans to thee;
Thou hast been a generous giver,
   Take this idle song from me.

The eighth stanza alludes to three friends named "Charles."
They were Charles Sumner, Charles Folsom, and Charles
Amory. Longfellow is also commemorated by a bust in the
Boston Public Library. See pages 32-33.

JOHN BOYLE O'REILLY

A photograph of part of this statue appears on the front
cover, top photograph.

Location: Intersection of The Fenway and Boylston Street.

If you're taking the T: The closest T station is Hynes Convention Center on the Green Line. Exit on Massachusetts Avenue. Go left for half a block. Turn right on Boylston Street. Follow Boylston Street for a block. At the traffic light, Boylston Street intersects The Fenway. The memorial is straight ahead.

If you're driving: Park on or near Boylston Street. If you need a GPS location, enter 1154 Boylston Street, Boston, which is the Massachusetts Historical Society. Once you have parked, stand on the MHS steps with your back to the building. To the left, across The Fenway, is the memorial.

This double-sided memorial to John Boyle O'Reilly, an Irish poet, is out of the way and well worth visiting. It's hidden in plain view because it presents the simpler reverse side to motorists on the road called The Fenway. Only walkers, runners, and cyclists can view the magnificent front. And only those who linger, such as lovers, can really appreciate the site, which is more than a statue. Daniel Chester French, the eminent American sculptor, designed the statues and bust. (He also designed the bronze doors to the Boston Public Library. See pages 25-26.) The architect C. Howard Walker designed the rest of the memorial, including the site.

The Fenway side of the memorial includes a granite bust of O'Reilly, carved designs of Irish knots (which continue on the other side), and an inscription:

John Boyle
O'Reilly
1844–1890
Poet Patriot
Orator

Above O'Reilly's head are two mythical creatures resembling seahorses with wings. They appear to have shamrocks on their heads and tails.

O'Reilly was born and grew up in Ireland, where he was arrested for his nationalist activities. He was imprisoned in Australia, but escaped. He made his way to America in 1869 and settled in Boston. He rose to became editor of *The Pilot*, the newspaper of the Roman Catholic Archdiocese.

On the river side of the memorial is French's bronze statue of three figures. It is called *Erin and Her Sons, Courage and Poetry*. The middle figure is Erin—Ireland. On her chest, she wears the relief image of a harp, a symbol of Ireland. She is weaving a laurel.

The male figure on the left is Courage. He is dressed militarily: in a knobbed helmet, high-laced toeless shoes, and what may be a cuff bracelet on his upper left arm. From a belt across his shoulder hangs a short sword, which is behind him.

Courage holds oak leaves. Across his lap lies a staff, possibly a small oak branch, cast in bronze to appear broken on the left side. On the right side, the staff, which might be a flagstaff, ends, possibly because the statute has been vandalized. The drapery in Courage's lap might be a flag.

The male figure on the right is Poetry. Poetry is nearly nude, draped only on his groin. He has angel's wings, and holds a lyre made from a turtle shell. (The lyre is supposed to have five strings, but vandals have left it with three.) The lyre is a classical symbol of poetry, possibly because the ancient Greeks played lyres to accompany their recitation of poetry.

Poetry leans with his long hair on Erin's arm. He reaches under Erin's left arm and hands her something small and curved.

The inscribed plaque under Erin reads in all capital letters: "Poetry and Patriotism give of their laurel and oak from which Erin weaves a wreath for her heroes." (The inscription refers to "Poetry and Patriotism," but the statue's name includes the words "Poetry" and "Courage.") In the lower right corner of the plaque are two wreaths in low relief and—look closely—two shamrocks.

Title: *Erin and Her Sons, Courage and Poetry*
Artist:
  Daniel Chester French
Medium: Bronze, granite
Date: 1896

Under Courage's right foot, the sculptor signed his work "Daniel French 1896." On the opposite side, under Poetry, appear these words in all capitals: "Cast by Henry Bonnard Bronze Co. 1896."

Erin gazes at the ground, not the viewer, in a pose that French used in other of his works. Poetry looks at the viewer. Courage looks resolutely into the near distance.

The statue is set in a miniature park with two curving stone benches. (This kind of bench is called an "exedra.") The traffic can make it a noisy site. From here you can see the Prudential Building and the CITGO sign in Kenmore Square. Here are two poems by O'Reilly, both in their entirety.

The White Rose
by John Boyle O'Reilly

The red rose whispers of passion,
  And the white rose breathes of love;
Oh, the red rose is a falcon,
  And the white rose is a dove.

But I send you a cream-white rosebud
  With a flush on its petal tips;
For the love that is purest and sweetest
  Has a kiss of desire on the lips.

Distance
by John Boyle O'Reilly

The world is large, when its weary leagues two loving hearts divide;
But the world is small, when your enemy is loose on the other side.

A bust of O'Reilly also appears in the Boston Public Library. For information about it and one other O'Reilly poem, see page 35. For information about a bas-relief silhouette of O'Reilly in Charlestown, see page 169.

If you're continuing to the Kahlil Gibran Memorial: *It is one station away on the T. Go to Hynes Convention Center Station (reverse the walking directions on page 83) and take any train inbound to Copley Square Station.*

If you want to walk. Return to Boylston Street. Walk until you reach Boylston and Dartmouth Streets, which is one corner of Copley Square. Continue with the directions below.

KAHLIL GIBRAN

Location: Dartmouth Street, Copley Square, opposite the entrance to the Boston Public Library.

If you're taking the T: The closest T stations are Copley Square on the Green Line and Back Bay on the Orange Line.

If you're driving: Park in or near Copley Square.

Make your way to Dartmouth Street, across the street from the front of the Boston Public Library's McKim building, the side with the statues in front. The memorial to Kahlil Gibran is free-standing, on what looks like a low speaker's podium, in Copley Square facing Trinity Church.

Title: *Kahlil Gibran Memorial*
Artist: Kahlil Gibran
  (nephew of the poet)
Medium: Bronze, granite
Date: 1977

The bronze plaque on this simple memorial depicts Kahlil Gibran with flowing hair and a hand resting on a book titled *The Prophet,* his most famous work. Boughs of a Lebanese cedar sweep toward him. The plaque gives his name and the years of his life, 1883–1931, and designates him as a poet and painter.

Gibran was born in Lebanon. His family left in 1895 when he was 12 and settled in Boston's South End. At one point in his young life, he visited the Boston Public Library every week.

The slanted stone next to the bronze plaque reads:

Kahlil Gibran • a native of Besharri Lebanon • found literary and artistic sustenance in the Denison Settlement House • the Boston Public Schools and the Boston Public Library • A grateful city acknowledges the greater harmony among men and strengthened universality of spirit given by Kahlil Gibran to the people of the world in return.

On the front vertical plane of the stone base is this quotation: "'It was in my heart to help a little because I was helped much.'" On the rear is carved: "Dedicated September • 25 • 1977."

The memorial was designed by his nephew, who shares his name. He signed the bronze plaque in the lower right corner, K. G. Gibran, and copyrighted it 1977.

Here are two excerpts from *The Prophet*.

And a woman who held a babe against her bosom said, Speak to us of Children.
　　And he said:
　　Your children are not your children.
　　They are the sons and daughters of Life's longing for itself.
　　They come through you but not from you,
　　And though they are with you, yet they belong not to you.

　　You may give them your love but not your thoughts.

For they have their own thoughts.
You may house their bodies but not their souls,
For their souls dwell in the house of tomorrow, which you
cannot visit, not even in your dreams.
You may strive to be like them, but seek not to make them
like you.
For life goes not backward nor tarries with yesterday.
You are the bows from which your children as living arrows
are sent forth.
The archer sees the mark upon the path of the infinite,
and He bends you with His might that

His arrows may go swift and far.
Let your bending in the archer's hand be for gladness;
For even as he loves the arrow that flies,
so He loves also the bow that is stable.

....

Then a ploughman said, Speak to us of Work.
And he answered, saying:
You work that you may keep pace with the earth and the
soul of the earth.
For to be idle is to become a stranger unto the seasons,
and to step out of life's procession, that marches in
majesty and proud submission towards the infinite.

When you work you are a flute through whose heart the
whispering of the hours turns to music.
Which of you would be a reed, dumb and silent, when all
else sings together in unison?

Always you have been told that work is a curse and labour a misfortune.

But I say to you that when you work you fulfil a part of earth's furthest dream, assigned to you when the dream was born,

And in keeping yourself with labour you are in truth loving life,

And to love life's labour is to be intimate with life's inmost secret.

But if in your pain you would call birth an affliction and the support of the flesh a curse written upon your brow, than I answer that naught but the sweat of your brow shall wash away that which is written.

You have been told that life is darkness, and in your weariness you echo what was said by the weary.

And I say that life is indeed darkness save when there is urge,

And all urge is blind save when there is knowledge,

And all knowledge is vain save when there is work,

And all work is empty save when there is love;

And when you work with love you bind yourself to yourself, and to one another, and to God.

And what is it to work with love?

It is to weave the cloth with threads drawn from your own heart, even as if your beloved were to wear that cloth.

It is to build a house with affection, even as if your beloved were to dwell in that house.

It is to sow seeds with tenderness and reap the harvest with joy, even as if your beloved were to eat the fruit.

It is to charge all things you fashion with a breath of your own spirit,

And to know that all the blessed dead are standing about you and watching.

Often have I heard you say, as if speaking in sleep, "He who works in marble, and finds the shape of his own soul in the stone, is nobler than he who ploughs the soil. And he who seizes the rainbow to lay it on a cloth in the likeness of man, is more than he who makes the sandals for our feet."

But I say, not in sleep but in the over- wakefulness of noontide, that the wind speaks not more sweetly to the giant oaks than to the least of all the blades of grass.

And he alone is great who turns the voice of the wind into a song made sweeter by his own loving.

Work is love made visible

And if you cannot work with love but only with distaste, it is better that you should leave your work and sit at the gate of the temple and take alms of those who work with joy.

For if you bake bread with indifference, you bake a bitter bread that feeds but half man's hunger.

And if you grudge the crushing of the grapes, your grudge distills a poison in the wine

And if you sing though as angels, and love not the singing, you muffle man's ears to the voices of the day and the voices of the night.

Questions

Do you agree with Gibran's thoughts on children and work?

As a parent or as a former child, do you agree that your children are not your children, that they are with you, yet they belong not to you?

Do you agree that work is love made visible?

Nearby, a poem excerpt is carved into stone that most people walk on without noticing.

With your back to the Boston Public Library, go left. At the corner, turn right on Boylston Street. You'll walk on seven rows of square designs set into the pavement. Past the rows of squares is a long thin piece of stone. If you reach the map of the Boston Marathon route, you've gone a few steps too far.

The poem excerpt reads:

> One equal temper of heroic hearts,
> Made weak by time and fate, but strong in will
> To strive, to seek, to find, and not to yield.
>   Tennyson, "Ulysses"

These are the last three lines of Alfred, Lord Tennyson's poem "Ulysses." To the left of the quotation is a logo of the Boston Athletic Association, which sponsors the Boston Marathon. To the right is the signature of John Hancock, the Massachusetts revolutionary who, among other things, signed the Declaration of Independence. His signature is the logo of John Hancock Financial, a corporate sponsor of the marathon.

If you're continuing to the Phillis Wheatley statue: Follow the directions in the third paragraph below, starting with "Facing the Boston Public Library."

PHILLIS WHEATLEY

A photograph of part of this statue appears on the back cover, in the middle. The photograph is tilted.

Location: Commonwealth Avenue, between Fairfield and Gloucester Streets, opposite 256 Commonwealth Avenue.

If you're taking the T: The closest T station is Copley Square on the Green Line. Leave the station and go to the closest intersection, which is Boylston and Dartmouth Streets. Facing the Boston Public Library, go right on Dartmouth Street. At the second street, which is Commonwealth Avenue, cross two lanes of vehicle traffic and turn left onto the boulevard. It's called the Commonwealth Avenue Mall. (That's "mall" as in "promenade," not "shopping mall."). Walk two blocks. After you cross Fairfield Street, the memorial will be in front of you.

If you're driving: Park near the intersection of Commonwealth Avenue and Fairfield Street or Gloucester Street. If you're using GPS, enter 256 Commonwealth Avenue, Boston.

A statue of the poet Phillis Wheatley is part of the Boston Women's Memorial 2003. The other two women depicted are Lucy Stone and Abigail Adams. Although this book focuses on poets and poetry, it will discuss all three women for two reasons. They are grouped to be in "conversation" with each other, as the sculptor has put it. Thus, Wheatley can't fairly be discussed alone. And the Boston Women's Memorial 2003 has not been written about in detail. The best discussion is an essay by the sculptor, which begins on page 99.

The pedestal gives Wheatley's name and the years of her life, 1753–1784, and then states:

> Born in West Africa and sold as a slave from the ship *Phillis* in colonial Boston, she was a literary prodigy whose *Poems on Various Subjects, Religious and Moral,* was the first book published by an African writer in America.

Wheatley's owners named her for the ship that transported her. Her sculpted image wears a bonnet and shell choker necklace. She holds a quill delicately and holds her left index finger to her cheek pensively. She and the other two women are 1.2 times life size.

Be sure to read excerpts from a letter by Wheatley that is carved into the pedestal serving as her writing surface. On vertical planes of the pedestal are excerpts from two poems. The complete poems follow.

On Imagination
by Phillis Wheatley

THY various works, imperial queen, we see,
How bright their forms! how deck'd with pomp by thee!
Thy wond'rous acts in beauteous order stand,
And all attest how potent is thine hand.

From *Helicon's* refulgent heights attend,
Ye sacred choir, and my attempts befriend:
To tell her glories with a faithful tongue,
Ye blooming graces, triumph in my song.

Now here, now there, the roving *Fancy* flies,
Till some lov'd object strikes her wand'ring eyes,
Whose silken fetters all the senses bind,
And soft captivity involves the mind.

Imagination! who can sing thy force?
Or who describe the swiftness of thy course?
Soaring through air to find the bright abode,
Th' empyreal palace of the thund'ring God,
We on thy pinions can surpass the wind,
And leave the rolling universe behind:
From star to star the mental optics rove,
Measure the skies, and range the realms above.
There in one view we grasp the mighty whole,
Or with new worlds amaze th' unbounded soul.

Though *Winter* frowns to *Fancy's* raptur'd eyes
The fields may flourish, and gay scenes arise;
The frozen deeps may break their iron bands,
And bid their waters murmur o'er the sands.
Fair *Flora* may resume her fragrant reign,
And with her flow'ry riches deck the plain;
Sylvanus may diffuse his honours round,
And all the forest may with leaves be crown'd:

Show'rs may descend, and dews their gems disclose,
And nectar sparkle on the blooming rose.

  Such is thy pow'r, nor are thine orders vain,
O thou the leader of the mental train:
In full perfection all thy works are wrought,
And thine the sceptre o'er the realms of thought.
Before thy throne the subject-passions bow,
Of subject-passions sov'reign ruler Thou;
At thy command joy rushes on the heart,
And through the glowing veins the spirits dart.

  Fancy might now her silken pinions try
To rise from earth, and sweep th' expanse on high;
From *Tithon's* bed now might *Aurora* rise,
Her cheeks all glowing with celestial dies,
While a pure stream of light o'erflows the skies.
The monarch of the day I might behold,
And all the mountains tipt with radiant gold,
But I reluctant leave the pleasing views,
Which *Fancy* dresses to delight the *Muse*;
Winter austere forbids me to aspire,
And northern tempests damp the rising fire;
They chill the tides of *Fancy's* flowing sea,
Cease then, my song, cease the unequal lay.

Here is the second poem.

To the Right Honourable WILLIAM, Earl of DARTMOUTH, His Majesty's Principal Secretary of State for North America, &c.

by Phillis Wheatley

HAIL, happy day, when, smiling like the morn,
Fair Freedom rose *New-England* to adorn:
The northern clime beneath her genial ray,
Dartmouth, congratulates thy blissful sway:
Elate with hope her race no longer mourns,
Each soul expands, each grateful bosom burns,
While in thine hand with pleasure we behold
The silken reins, and *Freedom's* charms unfold.
Long lost to realms beneath the northern skies
She shines supreme, while hated faction dies:
Soon as appear'd the *Goddess* long desir'd,
Sick at the view, she languish'd and expir'd;
Thus from the splendors of the morning light
The owl in sadness seeks the caves of night.

No more, *America*, in mournful strain
Of wrongs, and grievance unredress'd complain,
No longer shalt thou dread the iron chain,
Which wanton *Tyranny* with lawless hand
Had made, and with it meant t' enslave the land.

Should you, my lord, while you peruse my song,
Wonder from whence my love of *Freedom* sprung,
Whence flow these wishes for the common good,
By feeling hearts alone best understood,

I, young in life, by seeming cruel fate
Was snatch'd from *Afric's* fancy'd happy seat:
What pangs excruciating must molest,
What sorrows labour in my parent's breast?
Steel'd was that soul and by no misery mov'd
That from a father seiz'd his babe belov'd:
Such, such my case. And can I then but pray
Others may never feel tyrannic sway?

      For favours past, great Sir, our thanks are due,
And thee we ask thy favours to renew,
Since in thy pow'r, as in thy will before,
To sooth the griefs, which thou did'st once deplore.
May heav'nly grace the sacred sanction give
To all thy works, and thou for ever live
Not only on the wings of fleeting *Fame*,
Though praise immortal crowns the patriot's name,
But to conduct to heav'ns refulgent fane,
May fiery coursers sweep th' ethereal plain,
And bear thee upwards to that blest abode,
Where, like the prophet, thou shalt find thy God.

The carved biography for Lucy Stone notes that she lived
from 1818 to 1893 and states:

Born in Brookfield, she was one of the first Massachu-
setts women to graduate from college. She was an ardent
abolitionist, a renowned orator, and the founder of the
Woman's Journal, the foremost women's suffrage publica-
tion of its era.

The light gray granite is carved with an excerpt from Stone's writing in the *Woman's Journal* and one of her speeches.

The biography for Abigail Adams notes that she lived from 1744 to 1818 and states:

> Born in Weymouth, Massachusetts, she was the wife of the second president of the United States and the mother of the sixth. Her letters establish her as a perceptive social and political commentator and a strong voice for women's advancement.

Excerpts from two of her letters are carved into the light gray granite. One excerpt is fittingly about statues: "So rapid have been the changes: that...we are left like statues gazing at what we can neither fathom, or comprehend."

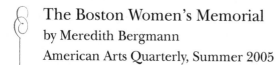

The Boston Women's Memorial
by Meredith Bergmann
American Arts Quarterly, Summer 2005

In 1992 over 100 people met at the Old South Meeting House to discuss the under-representation of women among Boston's public statues. A task force that became a site committee for a Women's Memorial chose three inspiring women — Abigail Adams, Lucy Stone and Phillis Wheatley — and secured the last empty memorial site on the Commonwealth Avenue Mall. The theme uniting the three women was that all had an impact on the idea of justice in our society through their writing, and this theme would be linked to educational programs. This part of the process, with many fervent discussions, took six years. Their next step was to select an artist, and to do that they had to formulate what they wanted that artist to achieve. Public art originates with a call for help with a group's expression. The group may issue an overt challenge to an artist to resolve contradictions or heal civic wounds, but the unspoken challenge is to the artist to create a work that has the power of what might be called "private" art, the kind the artist is driven to create only by the private urgencies of her or his own psyche. Every group hopes to commission a great work, for only art that arouses a passionate response is likely to bring much nourishment to the community it is intended to serve. We tend to believe that powerful art emanates from the aroused passions of the artist, and the public process must meet the both public's needs and the artist's.

At the first meeting I attended as a competition finalist, the site committee challenged us to design a contemporary work that would not be in conflict with the beautifully preserved nineteenth-century environment of Commonwealth Avenue Mall. This avenue of brick and brownstone townhouses, stone churches and dormitories has no commerce, no advertising. A progression of monuments, all to men, occupied a central promenade lined with elm trees. The formal vocabulary of these monuments — bronze upon inscribed stone — appealed to both my sense of order and my sense of humor. There was something about the seriousness of this commission, reminiscent of the "moral earnestness" that characterized monument-building in the nineteenth century, that earned my deepest respect (for the committee's passionate sense of need and neglect) and yet provoked in me an answering need to critique that sense of entitlement, to leaven that earnestness with wit and to try to combine beauty and idealism with the facts of life. This attitude comes in part from my artistic education and a lot from being a woman.

To my surprise, I drew inspiration and encouragement for my independent attitude from the words of Adams, Stone and Wheatley as I began to research them. Adams wrote to her husband during one of the long separations, for reasons of State, that characterized their marriage: "O, Why was I born with so much Sensibility and why possessing it have I so often been call'd to struggle with it?" For each of these women, life was a passionate struggle against both the external controls of society and the internal limitations of their own imaginations, conducted amidst a host of chores and cares: making soap or melting down spoons to cast bullets, nursing and burying children, defending their husbands' reputations and begging for subscribers. Reading their vivid words, I realized that this struggle was the story about women that I wanted to tell.

I studied the existing monuments along the Mall and decided that the formal symbols for remembrance, heroism and stature had to be used in a new way, for women. Each woman, like the men already memorialized, would be sculpted in bronze, larger than life, and have a tall granite pedestal with her words inscribed on it. I suddenly realized that I could portray the women as having come down off their pedestals, making a feminist metaphor literal and concrete. This would give the memorial a powerful symbolic structure that I could express both in words and in forms. Part of what defines contemporary art is its acute self-consciousness. My design makes reference to the moment when looming memorial sculpture of the nineteenth century was subverted by Rodin, who made a point of designing his Burghers of Calais to stand down on the common ground. But these women are not standing in heroic idleness, nor trudging in Rodin's "living rosary of suffering and sacrifice." They have come down to work, and thoughtfully put their skewed and tumbled pedestals to use. The design can be said, in all seriousness, to deconstruct and recycle traditional memorial design.

Each woman became emblematic of a stage of life and a kind of writing: imaginative, contemplative and activist. Wheatley sits in regal stillness but is charged with artistic energy, Adams is paused in activity and immersed in history, and Stone (who engaged most directly with the struggle for women's rights) is an embodiment of physical and moral strength. Each figure is posed in relation to her pedestal in a unique way that adds to her portrait. Stone has attempted to subdue and steer her pedestal, Adams leans in companionable, almost spousal co-existence on hers, and Wheatley has made hers into a desk, the object that symbolizes the privacy that she won with her talent while still a slave. I placed them around the circle, each absorbed in her work, with quotations or biographies readable from any angle to encourage visitors to compare their ideas and actions and to form their own conversation among them.

My design won the competition in June of 1998. The first work that I did to refine the design before it was presented to the various city commissions was to stage a sculpture rehearsal on the Mall with three very tall women and three painted foam-core pedestals resting on a large circle of painted fabric, to test the scale. In my proposal I had written that I wanted the women to have pedestals, "which are second only to obelisks as symbols of male power, to use for their own ends of female creativity, activism and expression." It had been my original intention to contrast the pedestals with the figures: masculine/feminine, minimal/figurative. The committee was concerned that the pedestals, originally three simple rectangular blocks, were too large for the figures and "too blocky." The 78-inch-tall blocks seemed small enough outdoors, but still dismayed the committee as not seeming feminine enough.

A committee's comments seem to the artist, at first, to be asking for something simpler and duller — although everyone is delighted if the artist can make it better. I began, that day, to learn to hear the question behind the criticism, the disappointed incomprehension behind the attack and even the problematic relief behind the compliment. This process of interpretation led me to understand better the needs the memorial would have to satisfy, and challenged me to make the work richer and more interesting. In this case, I was able to see that, by making the blocks smaller and adding a base with moldings to each one I would increase the number of elements I could play with and give Wheatley's figure a seat. I redesigned Stone's pose, using the two elements to prolong her climb. Eventually it occurred to me to use the molding profile to form the schematic silhouette of a woman (based on the Venus of Willendorf) so that the architecture is truly feminized.

I made each sculpture at least three times: as a twelve-inch model, a three-foot model and then at the finished size of just over six feet tall. At each stage my ideas and work were tested before commissions and committees. Sometimes there were loud, passionate discussions of details, such as whether Abigail Adams could be portrayed without a hat.

When I made the three-foot-tall model and set it up to scale in my studio, I realized that I had given the three figures parity from above (it's easy to think in these terms when working with a small model as an object on a table), and oriented them so that each would occupy one-third of the circle and would look in three different directions, encouraging visitors to move around the circle and providing significant views from all angles. At half size, I reached the point where I could better simulate the experience of visiting the memorial from ground level. Only then did I realize how the site would determine the interpretation of my design: the traditional eastward orientation of the other statues along the Mall made the eastern entry the definitive approach. The figure of Wheatley was turned away from this approach, and the mass of her body and skirt faced away from it. I was concerned that this aspect of the design could be interpreted as showing less respect to Wheatley. I did not want to create anything that reflected the racism that continues to pervade our society. I hired a model, studied possible variations to the pose and swung the lower half of Wheatley's body around so that she could still plausibly sit and write but would show her familiar, iconic profile to the main approach. Besides bringing Wheatley into greater prominence, this change allowed the flowing drapery of her skirt to balance that of Stone's. I was careful to design her figure so that this change did not make any of the other approaches or angles of view less interesting. In fact, it's a far more beautiful and interesting sculpture.

I made other changes to the figures at full size, based on further research, comments by the committee that visited my studio, a visit from a descendant of Abigail Adams (which gave me a chance to study his face) and from seeing the work in its final scale. The costumes are only half-historical (and half goddess), but Adams's gown acquired a more historically accurate drape after a curator in Quincy gingerly took one of her dresses out of its archival tissue and held it up for me. I added more detail and ornament to her costume, and her signature corkscrew curls, only after her basic figure and face had enough formal strength and character to sustain that level of detail. Then I added more volume and deeper modeling to her shawl, to better match the strongly modeled drapery on the other two figures.

Abigail Adams initially seemed the most distant to me, perhaps because she is the one I learned about in childhood — so I made her the eldest. Her life was that of a mother and wife of enormous influence and fertility, a paradigm of maternal involvement. It was important to me to show her at a relatively happy age, before (as she believed) the prolonged sickness and death of her only daughter had "stamped with indelible furros [sic] your Mother's visage" and "written strange the feature o'er my face." Though grief has often been the lot of women, I chose the moment before the grief hit. She stands unbent like a strong tree, and her face is alert and questioning, with a hint of the loving humor that enlivens her letters.

Unlike Adams, who was portrayed many times by different artists, or Stone, who lived recently enough to be photographed and was famous enough to have sat for a marble bust, Phillis Wheatley was portrayed only once in her lifetime, in an extremely conventionalized profile engraved for her book of poetry. She is shown with kinky hair and round eyes, an implausibly high, flat forehead to signify a noble mind, studiously pursed lips and a thoughtfully melancholy pose, chin in hand. Although her poems relate bits of the story of her being stolen from her parents and sold into slavery, there is nothing like the confessional tone of today's poets in her pious couplets. Only in her descriptions of the potential of a free inner life could I experience a deep sense of recognition, when she expressed her ambition, yearning and sense of profound injustice in metaphors of soaring flight. In this case, the identification was profound: I had

to study poetry to read hers in context, and that led me
to take poetry classes and to writing poetry of my own.

I also searched each woman's writings for evidence of her
response to art, to creativity and to statues. Lucy Stone
experienced an epiphany in front of a statue, when she
visited Boston years before she was to settle there. She
saw Hiram Powers's Greek Slave, a white marble statue of
a young woman who was orphaned by the Turks during
the Greek Revolution of 1821–1830 and forced to stand
naked (against her will) on the auction block (or pedes-
tal). In part because it was a culturally acceptable, tasteful
nude, the Greek Slave became the first celebrity sculpture
in America, widely exhibited and reproduced. Stone told
her daughter: "there it stood in the silence, with fettered
hands and half-averted face — so emblematic of women.
I remember how the hot tears came to my eyes at the
thought of the millions of women who must be freed...
it took hold of me like Samson upon the gates of Gaza."
That night she began to speak for women's rights and
when scolded for neglecting her anti-slavery topic, replied:
"I was a woman before I was an abolitionist." I love this
story, in part, because when I look at that statue I can't —
and most museumgoers nowadays can't — see what she
saw. In honor of this instance of the power of sculpture
to change the world, I made a brooch for Stone's bodice
with a tiny profile of the head of the Greek Slave.

From the beginning of this process I tried to immerse
myself in this material, believing that only by somehow
making it my own and speaking it fluently would I be
able to convey the quality of women's struggle for libera-

tion and achievement. The message of the memorial, I believe, is that because great women have had to struggle against both external and internal limitations while leading lives biologically determined to center around the needs of other people, they have a great deal to teach us about leading balanced but uncompromising lives. They combined unrelenting persistence with humor, devotion to their work with rich personal relationships, enormous energy with tenderness, anger with strategy, and faith that led them beyond life's tragedies. I tried to make every part of the memorial embody this message.

My only serious regret is that the budget would not cover the cost of the blood-red African granite I wanted to use as a pavement, as a reference to the blood shed by women in life-affirming ways and to honor Phillis Wheatley and the many African-Americans imported from Africa, like stone or any other goods, in the holds of ships. The floor of the memorial is a mild reddish-brown stone that deepens to blood-color only in the rain.

After the Memorial was unveiled in 2003, someone began leaving bouquets of flowers at Abigail Adams's feet, and then for days people would move the flowers around among bronze fingers and behind bronze ears. Right before the first snow a sweater was left draped around Lucy Stone's shoulders. I've watched children climb onto Phillis Wheatley's pedestal, stare into her eyes and touch her nose in wonder, and passersby stop to see the figures and then step intimately close to trace the carved quotations, closing the distance between legend and life.

All three figures have a two-part pedestal. The base is dark gray, almost black, and has a deep molding. The block is light gray. Adams leans against the gray block, which is stacked on the dark gray base. If it were a traditional statue, she'd be standing on the gray block.

The pedestals for the other two figures are deconstructed. Wheatley sits on the dark gray base and uses the light gray block, which is tipped on its long side, as a desk. Stone leans on the light gray block, which is also tipped on its side, and extends her feet behind her onto the dark gray base.

> **Title:** *The Boston Women's Memorial 2003*
> **Artist:** Meredith Bergmann
> **Medium:** Bronze and New England granite
> **Date:** 2003

Questions

The sculptor wrote that she placed the three figures around the circle to encourage visitors to compare their ideas and acts and to create conversation among them. Do you have comparisons of their ideas and acts? Do their ideas and acts inspire any of yours?

What jewelry does each figure wear?

What is common about what each figure holds?

What would you say in a poem, a speech, or a letter to Wheatley, Stone, or Adams?

> **A plaque about Wheatley is mounted in Chinatown. See pages 161-162 for its location and text.**

If you're continuing to the September 11 memorial, called the Garden of Remembrance 9/11, it is one station away on the T, near the Arlington Station. Go to Copley Square Station (reverse the walking directions on page 93) and take any inbound train for one station. Follow the signs to the Public Garden. You'll exit at the corner of Boylston and Arlington Streets. With the Public Garden on your right, walk on Arlington Street. You'll come to an entrance opposite Newbury Street, where Newbury Street intersects Arlington Street without crossing it. Enter the Public Garden and take an immediate right. If you need a GPS location, enter 17 Arlington Street, Boston, which is roughly across the street from the entrance to the Public Garden.

If you want to walk: Reverse direction and walk on Commonwealth Avenue toward Fairfield Street. When you get to Arlington Street, cross it, and turn right. The Public Garden will be on the left. Follow the directions in the paragraph above starting with "You'll come to an entrance."

THE GARDEN OF REMEMBRANCE 9/11

Location: The Public Garden, near the intersection of Arlington and Newbury Streets.

If you're taking the T: The closest T station is Arlington on the Green Line. Follow the directions above starting with "Follow the signs to the Public Garden."

If you're walking: Enter the Public Garden opposite Newbury Street, where Newbury Street intersects Arlington Street without crossing it. Enter the Public Garden and take an immediate right.

If you're driving: Park near the Public Garden, such as in the Boston Common Garage. If you need a GPS location, enter 17 Arlington Street, Boston, which is roughly across the street from the entrance to the Public Garden. Follow the directions in the previous paragraph.

Title: *Garden of Remembrance 9/11*	
Artist: Victor Walker	
Medium: Granite	
Date: 2011	

The Garden of Remembrance 9/11 is a memorial to people with ties to Massachusetts who died in the terrorist attacks on September 11, 2001. A curving band of granite has 206 inscribed names.

Carved into the granite that is set into the ground is this text:

> Time touches all more gently here,
> here where man has said, No;
> trees and grass, and flowers will remain;
> where the first-born sometimes sees
> his father's father's eyes
> reflected in the shallow pool;
> feels an ancient heart beat
> in the palm of his hand
> pressed against a willow;
> in seeking comfort, seeking shade
> lies beneath the golden leaf elm
> watching swanboats glide in season

From Boston and Sea Poems
Lawrence Homer, Poet Laureate

It is unclear whether the memorial reproduces the entire poem or an excerpt. When snow or ice is on the ground, it can cover or obscure the poem.

Question

What do you think is the connection between the poem and a memorial to people who died on September 11?

If you're continuing to the Edgar Allan Poe statue, the easiest way is to walk; it is between two T stops. Make your way to the walking path that runs parallel to Boylston Street. Walk to the next intersection. The Poe statue is kitty-corner.

EDGAR ALLAN POE

A photograph of this statue appears on the back cover, in the upper right.

Location: Corner of Arlington Street and Charles Street South. The closest street address is 2 Park Plaza, which you can use for GPS. (The intersection is also called Edgar Allan Poe Square, although that designation might not work for GPS. A very close intersection is Arlington and Carver Streets.)

If you're taking the T: The memorial is between two T stations on the Green Line, Arlington Station and Boylston Station. If you're using the Arlington Station, follow the signs to the Public Garden. You'll exit at the corner of Boylston and Arlington Streets. Continue on Boylston Street with the Public Garden on your left. Walk to the next intersection. The Poe statue is kitty-corner. If you're using Boylston Station, when you emerge above ground, continue walking ahead to the intersection of Tremont and Boylston Streets. Cross Boylston Street and go right. The Edgar Allan Poe statue is at the next major intersection, on the left.

Edgar Allan Poe was born in Boston in 1809 and had many later ties to it, but he had a contentious relationship with the city. He considered it provincial and its people small-minded. He referred to Bostonians as "Frogpondians," thereby reducing an entire city to a small pond on Boston Common inhabited by small croaking creatures. As the plaque on the nearby building states, the statue depicts Poe "returning to Boston. Just off the train, he is walking south: away from the Frog Pond and toward 62 Carver Street, where his parents were living around the time he was born. With a trunk full of ideas and worldwide success, he is finally coming home." Sixty-two Carver Street, which was nearby and was Poe's probable birthplace, no longer exists.

The statue—one of the best pieces of public art in Boston —features Poe's distinctive, even iconic, face. It is 5 feet 8 inches tall—Poe's height—and is at ground level with no pedestal. As its sculptor, Stefanie Rocknak, has said, "This isn't heroic size. I wanted people to relate to him as a human being. However, his reputation has certainly gotten bigger than most of us enjoy. That's why the raven is oversize."

A raven springs out of his trunk; Poe's poem "The Raven" is probably his most famous. Spilling out of Poe's trunk is a human heart—his story "The Tell-Tale Heart" is probably his most famous—and manuscript pages. "The Raven" appears below, as does a tiny excerpt from "The Tell-Tale Heart."

Trailing behind him are six pages set into the pavement bricks. If they're under snow or ice, or your eyesight or agility doesn't allow you to view the pages, here are the texts. Beginning with the one closest to the statue, the pages proceed in chronological order:

> "Villains!" I shrieked, "dissemble no more! I admit the deed! — tear up the planks! — here, here! — it is the beating of his hideous heart!"

From "The Tell-Tale Heart," first published in *The Pioneer*, a Boston literary magazine, in January 1843.

> *All* that we see or seem
> Is but a dream within a dream.

From "A Dream within a Dream," first published in *The Flag of Our Union*, a Boston newspaper, on March 31, 1849.

> The Bostonians are very well in their way. Their hotels are bad. Their pumpkin pies are delicious. Their poetry is not so good. Their Common is no common thing — and the duck-pond might answer — if its answer could be heard for the frogs.

From "Editorial Miscellany," *Broadway Journal*, a New York literary magazine, November 1, 1845.

I reach'd my home — my home no more —
For all was flown that made it so —
I pass'd from out its mossy door,
In vacant idleness of woe.

From "Tamerlane," included in Poe's first book, *Tamerlane and Other Poems by a Bostonian*, printed in Boston by Calvin F. S. Thomas in 1827.

Because I feel that, in the heavens above,
The angels, whispering to one another,
Can find, among their burning terms of love,
None so devotional as that of 'mother'—

From "Sonnet—To My Mother," first published in *The Flag of Our Union*, a Boston newspaper, on July 7, 1849.

"We want characters — characters, man — something novel—out of the way. We are wearied with this everlasting sameness. Come, drink! the wine will brighten your wits."

From "Hop-Frog," first published in *The Flag of Our Union*, a Boston newspaper, on March 7, 1849.

Here are two poems by Poe, including "The Raven."

Title: *Poe Returning to Boston*
Artist: Stefanie Rocknak
Medium: Bronze
Date: 2014

The Raven
by Edgar Allan Poe

Once upon a midnight dreary, while I pondered, weak and weary,
Over many a quaint and curious volume of forgotten lore –
While I nodded, nearly napping, suddenly there came a tapping,
As of some one gently rapping, rapping at my chamber door.
" 'Tis some visitor," I muttered, "tapping at my chamber door –
      Only this, and nothing more."

Ah, distinctly I remember it was in the bleak December;
And each separate dying ember wrought its ghost upon the floor.
Eagerly I wished the morrow; – vainly I had sought to borrow
From my books surcease of sorrow – sorrow for the lost Lenore –
For the rare and radiant maiden whom the angels name Lenore –
      Nameless *here* for evermore.

And the silken sad uncertain rustling of each purple curtain
Thrilled me – filled me with fantastic terrors never felt before;
So that now, to still the beating of my heart, I stood repeating,
" 'Tis some visitor entreating entrance at my chamber door –
Some late visitor entreating entrance at my chamber door; –
      This it is, and nothing more."

Presently my soul grew stronger; hesitating then no longer,
"Sir," said I, "or Madam, truly your forgiveness I implore;
But the fact is I was napping, and so gently you came rapping,
And so faintly you came tapping, tapping at my chamber door,
That I scarce was sure I heard you" – here I opened wide the door; –
      Darkness there, and nothing more.

Deep into that darkness peering, long I stood there wondering, fearing,
Doubting, dreaming dreams no mortals ever dared to dream before;
But the silence was unbroken, and the stillness gave no token,
And the only word there spoken was the whispered word, "Lenore?"
This I whispered, and an echo murmured back the word, "Lenore!"
    Merely this, and nothing more.

Back into the chamber turning, all my soul within me burning,
Soon again I heard a tapping somewhat louder than before.
"Surely," said I, "surely that is something at my window lattice;
Let me see, then, what thereat is, and this mystery explore –
Let my heart be still a moment and this mystery explore; –
    'Tis the wind and nothing more."

Open here I flung the shutter, when, with many a flirt and flutter,
In there stepped a stately Raven of the saintly days of yore;
Not the least obeisance made he; not a minute stopped or stayed he;
But, with mien of lord or lady, perched above my chamber door –
Perched upon a bust of Pallas just above my chamber door –
    Perched, and sat, and nothing more.

Then this ebony bird beguiling my sad fancy into smiling,
By the grave and stern decorum of the countenance it wore,
"Though thy crest be shorn and shaven, thou," I said, "art sure no craven,
Ghastly grim and ancient Raven wandering from the Nightly shore –
Tell me what thy lordly name is on the Night's Plutonian shore!"
    Quoth the Raven, "Nevermore."

Much I marvelled this ungainly fowl to hear discourse so plainly,
Though its answer little meaning – little relevancy bore;
For we cannot help agreeing that no living human being
Ever yet was blest with seeing bird above his chamber door –

Bird or beast upon the sculptured bust above his chamber door,
     With such name as "Nevermore."

But the raven, sitting lonely on the placid bust, spoke only
That one word, as if his soul in that one word he did outpour.
Nothing further then he uttered – not a feather then he fluttered –
Till I scarcely more than muttered, "Other friends have flown before –
On the morrow *he* will leave me, as my hopes have flown before."
     Then the bird said, "Nevermore."

Startled at the stillness broken by reply so aptly spoken,
"Doubtless," said I, "what it utters is its only stock and store
Caught from some unhappy master whom unmerciful Disaster
Followed fast and followed faster till his songs one burden bore –
Till the dirges of his Hope that melancholy burden bore
     Of "Never – nevermore."

But the Raven still beguiling all my fancy into smiling,
Straight I wheeled a cushioned seat in front of bird, and bust and door;
Then upon the velvet sinking, I betook myself to linking
Fancy unto fancy, thinking what this ominous bird of yore –
What this grim, ungainly, ghastly, gaunt and ominous bird of yore
     Meant in croaking "Nevermore."

This I sat engaged in guessing, but no syllable expressing
To the fowl whose fiery eyes now burned into my bosom's core;
This and more I sat divining, with my head at ease reclining
On the cushion's velvet lining that the lamplight gloated o'er,
But whose velvet-violet lining with the lamp-light gloating o'er,
     She shall press, ah, nevermore!

Then methought the air grew denser, perfumed from an unseen censer
Swung by seraphim whose foot-falls tinkled on the tufted floor.
"Wretch," I cried, "thy God hath lent thee – by these angels he
hath sent thee
Respite – respite and nepenthe, from thy memories of Lenore;
Quaff, oh quaff this kind nepenthe and forget this lost Lenore!"
    Quoth the Raven, "Nevermore."

"Prophet!" said I, "thing of evil! – prophet still, if bird or devil! –
Whether Tempter sent, or whether tempest tossed thee here ashore,
Desolate yet all undaunted, on this desert land enchanted –
On this home by Horror haunted – tell me truly, I implore –
Is there – *is* there balm in Gilead? – tell me – tell me, I implore!"
    Quoth the Raven, "Nevermore."

"Prophet!" said I, "thing of evil – prophet still, if bird or devil!
By that Heaven that bends above us – by that God we both adore –
Tell this soul with sorrow laden if, within the distant Aidenn,
It shall clasp a sainted maiden whom the angels name Lenore –
Clasp a rare and radiant maiden whom the angels name Lenore."
    Quoth the Raven, "Nevermore."

"Be that word our sign in parting, bird or fiend," I shrieked, upstarting –
"Get thee back into the tempest and the Night's Plutonian shore!
Leave no black plume as a token of that lie thy soul hath spoken!
Leave my loneliness unbroken! – quit the bust above my door!
Take thy beak from out my heart, and take thy form from off my door!"
    Quoth the Raven, "Nevermore."

And the Raven, never flitting, still is sitting, still is sitting
On the pallid bust of Pallas just above my chamber door;
And his eyes have all the seeming of a demon's that is dreaming,

And the lamp-light o'er him streaming throws his shadow on the floor;
And my soul from out that shadow that lies floating on the floor
    Shall be lifted – nevermore!

Annabel Lee
by Edgar Allan Poe

It was many and many a year ago,
  In a kingdom by the sea,
That a maiden there lived whom you may know
  By the name of Annabel Lee; –
And this maiden she lived with no other thought
  Than to love and be loved by me.
She was a child and *I* was a child,
  In this kingdom by the sea,
But we loved with a love that was more than love –
  I and my Annabel Lee –
With a love that the wingéd seraphs of Heaven
  Coveted her and me.

And this was the reason that, long ago,
  In this kingdom by the sea,
A wind blew out of a cloud by night
  Chilling my beautiful Annabel Lee;
So that her high-born kinsman came
  And bore her away from me,
To shut her up in a sepulchre
  In this kingdom by the sea.

The angels, not half so happy in Heaven,
  Went envying her and me;
Yes! that was the reason (as all men know,
  In this kingdom by the sea)
That the wind came out of the cloud, chilling
  And killing my Annabel Lee.

But our love it was stronger by far than the love
  Of those who were older than we –
  Of many far wiser than we –
And neither the angels in Heaven above
  Nor the demons down under the sea,
Can ever dissever my soul from the soul
Of the beautiful Annabel Lee: –

For the moon never beams without bringing me dreams
  Of the beautiful Annabel Lee;
And the stars never rise but I feel the bright eyes
  Of the beautiful Annabel Lee;
And so, all the night-tide, I lie down by the side
Of my darling, my darling, my life and my bride
  In the sepulchre there by the sea –
  In her tomb by the side of the sea.

Questions

Should a city honor former residents who disdained it?

Do you think that Poe would have preferred to be depicted as leaving Boston, rather than returning to it?

Do you agree with Poe that Bostonians' hotels are bad, their pumpkin pies are delicious, and their poetry, not so good?

Carver Street, where Poe was probably born, is several steps away. So is another plaque about him.

If you're facing the plaque on the building about the statue, continue on Boylston Street to your left. As you turn the corner, you'll see Carver Street, which is an alley. On the facade of 176 Boylston Street is an older plaque commemorating Poe.

If you're continuing to the sculpture called The Massachusetts Artifact: *It is one station away on the T, Park Street Station. Go to Boylston Station by walking on Boylston Street with the Boston Common on your left. When you get to the intersection of Boylston and Tremont Streets, cross Boylston Street and enter the Boylston station at the inbound entrance. Exit at Park Street Station. When you emerge above ground, make your way up the hill to the Massachusetts State House, the building with the golden dome. Then follow the directions two paragraphs below.*

If you want to walk: Cross Boylston Street to Boston Common. Make your way across the Common to the Massachusetts State House, the building with the golden dome.

When you get to the State House, go right. At the corner (Bowdoin Street), turn left. At the next corner, turn right onto Ashburton Place. One Ashburton Place is the tall office building that you first come to on your left.

This state government building is open only during business hours. So you can't visit it in the evening or on a weekend or holiday.

THE MASSACHUSETTS ARTIFACT

A photograph of part of this sculpture appears on the back cover, in the middle on the left.

Location: Lobby, John W. McCormack State Office Building, One Ashburton Place, Boston.

If you're taking the T: The closest station is Park Street on the Green and Red Lines. When you emerge above ground, make your way up the hill to the Massachusetts State House, the building with the golden dome. When you get to the State House, go right. At the corner (Bowdoin Street), turn left. At the next corner, turn right onto Ashburton Place. One Ashburton Place is the tall office building that you first come to on your left.

If you're driving: Make your way to Beacon Hill and find parking on the street or in a garage.

This state government building is open only during business hours. So you can't visit it in the evening or on a weekend or holiday.

This sculpture screen includes many plaques with the initials of Bay State personages, some famous, some obscure; the first sculpted depiction of the ducks in *Make Way for Ducklings*; stylized seals of some cities and towns—and stuff that the artist threw in there, like his cat, rendered in bronze.

The sculpture comprises many artifacts, but its creator titled it *The Massachusetts Artifact* in the singular. Sculptor Alfred M. Duca installed it in 1975, three years after the building opened. It is approximately 25 feet wide and 27 feet tall.

Although this book focuses on sites associated with poets and poetry, it discusses the entire *Massachusetts Artifact*, not only its references to poets. The reason is that *The Massachusetts Artifact* has not been written about in detail elsewhere.

The central theme of the sculpture, Duca wrote, was "an interpretation of the many facets of Massachusetts, its history, its prominent places, and things. The seals of cities and towns, legends of artifacts were to be interwoven with cryptic representations of names of individuals whose lives figured so prominently [i]n the history of Massachusetts and who were no longer among the living.

"In researching subjects and reviewing those submitted by the [Massachusetts Art] commission and others, I selected ones that provided for fair regional representation and allowed for a diverse balance of ethnic interests. Symbols describing or pictorializing the historic, institutional and cultural clusters were integrated alongside professions, crafts, trades, academics, etc. Figures of birds, barnyard animals, fish, [and] flowers are juxtaposed with design details reflecting quilting patterns, clipper ship flags, and stenciling. Ancient symbols representing water, lime,

Title: *The Massachusetts Artifact*
Artist: Alfred M. Duca
Medium: Bronze
Date: 1975

steel, wood, etc. peek out from between images of early grave stone markers—angel heads, skulls, sunrises, sunsets.

"Scampering throughout the various levels of the sculpture are heroes and legends of heroes, and spirited shapes intoning a sense of seasons...marshes...hills, and other influences, some seen, some felt, here a train, there a telephone...."

Duca added that the oval plaques are "cameo-like" and "heraldic." They form "layers symbolizing the pyramidal aspect of Government."

Duca noted that the rooster appeared throughout the sculpture and wrote, "The many kinds of rooster shapes that early artisans employed can be seen on the countless barns, church spires and town steeples of the state."

He wrote, "Keep looking and you will find references to ships, trains, telephones, a sextant, a captain's speaking horn, a dory, a schooner. There are symbols for sand clocks, electronics, fishing, [and] farming." (It is unclear where the symbols for sand clocks, fishing, and farming are.)

Duca's papers, which are in the Smithsonian Archives of American Art in Washington, D.C., reveal that the state considered publishing a booklet explaining this sculpture, artifact by artifact, and that Duca expected the state to do so. His papers contain a few inquiries from people about the meaning of *The Massachusetts Artifact*. But the state did not publish such a booklet. This is the first detailed explanation.

Duca's papers indicate that he tried to include Americans with roots in Germany, Greece, Italy, Portugal, France, Arab countries, Hispanic countries, Africa, and Asia, and Native Americans, American Jews, women, gays, and children. One document indicates his effort to include pilgrims, and people from the fields of architecture, art, music, letters, theater and entertainment, law, politics, public life, the military, medicine, science, philosophy, religion, education, and sports.

Duca's handwritten notes—which he probably prepared in expectation that the state would publish an explanatory booklet—review *The Massachusetts Artifact* starting from the bottom, designating them as Rows A through U. So this book does so as well. The references are from left to right.

Some designs are not explained in Duca's notes. They are merely decorative, as Alfred Duca's son Richard explained to me. Richard Duca, who is also a sculptor and worked on his father's commission, described the creative process as free-wheeling. "Friends would come by," he recalled, referring to the studio, "and say, 'Oh, put this in.'" And they did.

At the very bottom of the sculpture are three swimming ducks and two standing ones. They represent the ducklings in *Make Way for Ducklings*, the Robert McCloskey book set in Boston. Duca's sculpted tribute to the ducklings preceded

Nancy Schön's 1987 sculpture *Make Way for Ducklings* in the Public Garden by 12 years.

Row A *(bottom row)*

Greek symbol for light and life, according to Duca's notes.

Although the plaque looks as if it reads "T's," Duca's notes indicate that he intended "**Tis**," short for "Tisquantum." Tisquantum (?–1622) was a member of the Patuxet tribe who helped the Puritans. He was also called Squanto. On top of the abbreviated version of Tisquantum's name are what appears to be stylized feathers.

LMA: Louisa May Alcott (1832–1888) was a novelist. Her best-known work is *Little Women*, which is based on her childhood in Concord.

NW: Noah Webster (1758–1843) is best known as a lexicographer. A native of Connecticut, he lived in Massachusetts for about a decade.

CA: Crispus Attucks (c. 1723–1770), a man of African and Wampanoag heritage, was the first casualty of the Boston Massacre.

Seal of the **Town of Salem**. This rendition is highly stylized with the elements rearranged. The shape over the human figure is probably a parasol.

JA PM: John Alden (c. 1599–1687) and Priscilla Mullins (c. 1602–c. 1685) married each other in Plymouth Colony;

she became Priscilla Alden. They were the protagonists of Henry Wadsworth Longfellow's poem "The Courtship of Miles Standish." Connecting the letters *J* and *A* may be the top of a heart shape. The *P* may include the bottom of the heart.

Prince H: Prince Hall (c. 1735–1738 – 1807) was an African-American abolitionist.

WB: William Bradford (c. 1590–1657) was governor of Plymouth Colony.

Barnyard scene.

MS: Miles (or "Myles") Standish (c. 1584–1656) was the military commander of Plymouth Colony.

Seal of the **Town of Lowell**. This is a highly stylized and stripped-down rendition. The two house-like structures are mills or a mill. The actual seal depicts two smokestacks.

Row B

LJ: Lorenzo Jeffers (1892–1974) was a supreme sachem of the Wampanoag Tribe in Gay Head. Next to the initials are what appear to be stylized feathers. It is unclear what the triangular symbol represents. Although it looks like a tepee, Wampanoags did not live in tepees.

Captain's speaking horn, shipping flags, and the fore and aft of the schooner *Atlast*. (The *Atlast* was a schooner that the sculptor's son Richard and Richard's friends built in the 1970s.) The arrow pointing to a large E may symbolize a compass.

ET: Enoch Train (1801–1868) was one of Boston's leading merchant shipowners. Above his initials, a rectangle with a circle in it might be a depiction of paper money.

DS: Daniel Shays (c.1747–1825) was a farmer and Revolutionary War soldier. He was a leader of Shays's Rebellion, a populist uprising in Massachusetts from 1786 to 1787.

Fish weathervane.

Indian design.

Seal of the Town of Manchester, which officially became **Manchester-by-the-Sea** in 1989. This rendition is stylized. Notice the M above the ship.

Squirrel. The squirrel has no significance beyond being playful and typically New England, said Alfred Duca's son Richard.

Seal of the **Town of Plymouth**. The actual seal has kneeling figures in the quadrants.

OWH: Oliver Wendell Holmes, Sr. (1809–1894) was a doctor and man of letters. His son, Oliver Wendell Holmes, Jr., was a Supreme Court justice, but Duca's notes reveal that the initials refer to the father.

Street lamp.

Goose. The accounts that Mother Goose was a Bostonian have generally been discredited, but people still repeat that legend. Duca did not intend his goose to pay tribute to this legend; his son Richard said that it was meant to be simply a goose.

AH: Anne Hutchinson (1591–1643) was a Puritan religious leader who was tried for and convicted of heresy, and exiled from Massachusetts. (Her statue stands nearby in front of the State House.)

SA: Samuel Adams (1722–1803) was a revolutionary leader. (A statue of him stands outside Faneuil Hall.)

M: Massasoit (c. 1581–1661) was a sachem of the Wampanoag Tribe. On top of this name are what appear to be feathers.

Row C

WD: William Dawes (1745–1799) was among several people, the most famous being Paul Revere, who alerted the citizenry on the night of April 18, 1775 that British troops were marching into the countryside, leading to battles the next day in Concord and Lexington. To the right of the plaque with Dawes's initials is an urgent rider on a galloping horse. A document in Duca's papers suggests that the figure might be Paul Revere and not Dawes.

Seal of the **City of Springfield**. This rendition is somewhat stylized.

Squirrel.

AW: Artemas Ward (1727–1800) was a Revolutionary War major general and later a congressman.

Printed circuits represent the electronics industry—as of the 1970s.

Stonemason's mark.

PW: Peregrine White (1620–1704) was the first known English child born to Puritans in Massachusetts.

Telephone representing the communications industry. Duca's son Richard confirmed that his father was aware of and paid tribute to the role that Massachusetts played in the telephone's development, even though his notes do not indicate it. (A nearby monument, on Cambridge Street in front of the John F. Kennedy Federal Building and opposite 1 Center Plaza, reads: "Birthplace of the telephone. Here, on June 2, 1875, Alexander Graham Bell and Thomas A. Watson first transmitted sound over wires. The successful experiment was completed in a fifth floor garret at what was then 109 Court Street and marked the beginning of worldwide telephone service.")

JA: John Adams (1735–1826), born in Braintree, was the first vice president of the United States and the second president.

Detail from a **colonial burial stone**.

Train representing transportation.

Eagle wing. According to Duca's notes, this was the symbol of the Express Line Clipper Ships, which were built in Medford.

HK: Henry Knox (1750–1806) was a Revolutionary War military officer and later the first U.S. Secretary of War. Fort Knox, Kentucky is named for him. He was born in Boston. He participated in the Siege of Boston and the Battle of Bunker Hill. Two stars appear on the plaque.

Stencil pattern for chairs and trays.

MD: Mary Dyer (c. 1611–1660) was a Quaker hanged for violating a law banning Quakers from Massachusetts. (Her statue sits nearby in front of the State House.)

Engraving on an Indian birch bark container.

Row D

DMcK: Donald McKay (1810–1880) was the designer and builder of the clipper sailing ships. He lived in East Boston.

Wind, wave, and water.

Rooster weathervane.

Seal of the **Town of Fall River**. This rendition is slightly stylized. It includes a paddle boat, a sailing ship, and the town's motto "We'll Try."

JH: John Harvard (1607–1638) donated about 100 English pounds and his library, about 400 books, to what was then the new college in Cambridge, which was named after him.

The **Lion of Judah.** Richard Duca is fairly certain that his father intended this as a Jewish symbol.

PR: Paul Revere (1734–1818). To the left of Revere's initials are what appear to be a stylized steeple and lantern; above and to the right, are what appear to be two stylized steeples and lanterns. If they are what they appear to be, they refer to "One if by land, two if by sea," a line from Henry Wadsworth Longfellow's poem "Paul Revere's Ride."

Seals of the **Town of Edgartown** (top) and the **Town of Tisbury** (bottom), both on Martha's Vineyard.

Seal of the **Town of Gloucester**, which was Duca's hometown. This rendition is the least stylized of any of the municipal seals.

ED: Emily Dickinson was a poet who was born in Amherst and is called the Belle of Amherst.

FHL: Fitz Henry Lane (1804–1865) was a painter who was born in Gloucester, and lived and painted there and in Boston. (Duca's statue of Lane is in Gloucester.)

Row E

LTD: "Lord" Timothy Dexter (1748–1806) was an eccentric

businessman and writer in Newburyport. His initials are sur-mounted by a crown, whose significance is unclear.

CB: Clara Barton (1821–1912), the founder of the Red Cross, was born in North Oxford.

AL: Mother Ann Lee (1736–1784) was a Shaker leader who was active in Massachusetts and other states.

Grasshopper weathervane. This is supposed to be the famous grasshopper weathervane topping Faneuil Hall, according to Richard Duca. The grasshopper's pose in *The Massachusetts Artifact* is different from its pose in the actual weathervane.

James Otis (1725–1783), whose name is highly stylized, was a lawyer in Massachusetts. His acts and ideas influenced the Revolution.

RHG: Robert H. Goddard 1882–1945) is credited with designing and building the first liquid-fueled rocket. He performed his early experiments in the Worcester area.

Row F

Massachusetts state seal. This rendition is highly stylized, with its elements rearranged. The actual state seal contains these Latin words, "Ense petit placidam sub libertate quietem," which is usually translated as "By the sword we seek peace, but peace only under liberty." The first letters of each word in the Latin phrase, *E, P, P, S, L,* and *Q,* appear on this plaque, the *P* appearing only once.

Detail from a **quilting pattern**.

Weathervane.

RGS: Robert Gould Shaw (1837–1863) was the white commanding officer of the first all African-American regiment, the 54th Massachusetts Regiment. He was born in Boston. (The Robert Gould Shaw Memorial is nearby, on the Boston Common, opposite the State House.)

LS: Lemuel Shattuck (1793–1859) was a merchant, publisher, bookseller, and member of the Boston City Council and Massachusetts House of Representatives. (There is a slight chance that Duca intended "LS" to stand for "Lemuel Shaw" (1781–1861), who was a chief justice of the Massachusetts Supreme Judicial Court, instead of, or in addition to, Lemuel Shattuck.)

Studio patterns. Duca did not explain in his notes what he meant by studio patterns. According to his son Richard, they are decorative patterns.

Birds and flowers.

Row G

Pineapple (a symbol of hospitality).

Seal of the **Island of Nantucket**. Notice the whale.

PE: Prince Estabrook (c. 1741–1830), an African-American slave and a private in the Lexington Minutemen, was wounded during the Battles of Lexington and Concord.

NW: Norbert Wiener (1894–1964) was a mathematician and philosopher who taught at the Massachusetts Institute of Technology. This is the second "NW" on *The Massachusetts Artifact*; the first one, in Row A, is for Noah Webster.

Duca's notes for this artifact read in their entirety: "Symbol, A Riddle & Prof. Norbert Weiner [sic]." If the riddle has anything to do with Wiener's mathematical work, no one with a math background whom I have asked has been able to discern a mathematical riddle. This artifact might depict a chicken and, on top of it, an egg. Duca may have been referring to the philosophical riddle: Which came first, the chicken or the egg? If the bird is a chicken and the three squiggles below it represent a road, Duca may have been referring to the most famous riddle: Why did the chicken cross the road?

The next artifact may be an amalgamation of the seal of the **Town of Groton** and a **detail from a country newspaper**. A plow and the words "Faith" and "Labor" appear on the Groton seal. This artifact is a stylized rendition of the Groton seal, with one element missing. Meanwhile, the homestead and chicken that appear on this artifact do not appear on the Groton seal. According to Duca's notes, this artifact is a detail from a country paper. Thus, it may signify both Groton and a country newspaper.

PF: Peter Faneuil (1700–1743) was a merchant and philanthropist who donated Faneuil Hall to Boston.

Samuel: Samuel McIntyre (1757–1811) was an architect and craftsman who was born and worked in Salem. Depicted are a plane to smooth wood and probably an awl.

Symbol of the **bookbinder's trade**, according to Duca's notes. On the left may be a bookbinder's press (in the middle of the device is apparently an end view of a book) and on the right, a glue pot and brush. "**Ben**" probably stands for "Ben Franklin," who was born in Boston in 1705 or 1706, and lived here till he was 17.

JQA: John Quincy Adams (1767–1848) was born in Braintree and served as the sixth president of the United States.

Row H

DLD: Dorthea L. Dix (1802–1887) was a national advocate for indigent people who were mentally ill or insane. She helped create the first generation of insane asylums. She grew up in Worcester and Boston.

Seal of the **Town of Canton**. It is unknown why Duca chose Canton. The reasons he chose other localities whose seals he portrayed are obvious: Springfield and Worcester are the state's second and third largest cities. Lowell, Brockton, and Fall River were major industrial cities. Salem was a major shipping city; Plymouth is historic. But the reasons he chose most localities are not obvious. According to the sculptor's son Richard, people working on the sculpture chose seals based on geographic diversity, personal favorites, and what they portrayed, such as mills, which were important to Massachusetts's development.

JW: Joseph Warren (1741–1775) was a medical doctor and revolutionary leader. A major general in the Massachusetts militia, he was killed during the Battle of Bunker Hill.

Detail from a **colonial tombstone**.

Studio patterns.

EB: Edward Bellamy (1850–1898) was a socialist and author, best known for his novel *Looking Backwards.* He was born in Chicopee.

WEBD: W. E. B. DuBois (1868–1963) was a sociologist, historian, and civil rights activist. He was the first African-American to earn a doctorate at Harvard University. He was born in Great Barrington.

Electra, Duca's **cat**.

Row I

DW: Daniel Webster (1782–1852) was a U.S. senator from Massachusetts and twice the U.S. secretary of state.

PDW: Paul Dudley White (1886–1973) was a leading cardiologist. He was born in Roxbury.

Detail from a **quilting pattern**.

Seal of the **Town of Reading**. Notice the waterwheel on a mill.

Detail from a **weathervane**. It is unclear what the other design elements are.

eec: E. E. Cummings (1894–1962) was a prominent American poet. Cummings typically used lowercase letters in his poems and sometimes spelled his name all in lowercase—but not always. The lowercase initials in *The Massachusetts Artifact* reflect the spelling "e. e. cummings" that people generally used at the time that the sculpture was created. Scholars and publishers now generally spell his name "E. E. Cummings." He was born in Cambridge.

Detail from a **quilting pattern**.

BW: Benjamin Waterhouse was a co-founder of Harvard Medical School. His initials appear three times; it is unclear why.

Ancient symbol for **steel**. Duca's notes do not indicate who used this symbol and when, or why he paid tribute to steel, when Massachusetts is not well known for manufacturing it.

Seal of the **Town of Pittsfield**.

LP: Lydia Pinkham (1819–1883) formulated and sold herbal tonics to ease menstruation and menopause. Some modern feminists admire her because she distributed information about women's health. She was born and lived in Lynn.

Seal of the **City of Malden**. It depicts three lions.

JSC: John Singleton Copley (1737 or 1738–1815) was a painter who lived and worked in Boston; he was probably born here too. (His statue stands in Boston's Copley Square, which is named for him.)

WPGM: William Thomas Green Morton was a dentist who first publicly demonstrated the use of ether as anesthesia for a surgery patient. The demonstration was at Massachusetts General Hospital. He was born in Charlton. The surgeon was John C. Warren, whose initials appear in Row P. (This plaque contains one of the few errors in the piece: Morton's initials should be "WTGM," not "WPGM.")

Tern.

Crewelwork (embroidery) of a **peacock** on a coverlet.

WLG: William Lloyd Garrison (1805–1879) was a social reformer best known for his work to abolish slavery. He published the abolitionist newspaper *The Liberator* in Boston. (His statue stands on the Commonwealth Avenue Mall between Dartmouth and Exeter Streets.)

Detail from a **quilting pattern**.

Row K

Bird.

MBE: Mary Baker Eddy (1805–1879) founded Christian Science. She lived in various localities in Massachusetts.

SEM: Samuel Eliot Morison (1887–1976) was a rear admiral and Pulitzer Prize–winning historian. He was born in Boston. (His statue sits on the Commonwealth Avenue Mall between Exeter and Fairfield Streets.)

Pressed leaves.

WG: Walter Gropius (1883–1969) was an architect who lived and designed buildings in Massachusetts.

Scrimshaw artifact, sail seam sealer, according to Duca's notes. This may be a tool to seal the seams of sails, carved from whalebone. The top resembles a fist; the bottom, a four-masted ship between brackets. It is unknown whether Duca intended the resemblances.

Bell.

FLO: Frederick Law Olmsted (1822–1903) was a pioneer of American landscape architecture. He designed Boston's Emerald Necklace. His firm was in Brookline.

Weathervane **monster**.

WB: William Brewster (c. 1566–1644) was a *Mayflower* passenger and religious leader in Plymouth Colony. The significance of a design flourish next to his initials, resembling a dagger, is unknown.

Seal of the **City of Attleboro**. It is unknown what the H and A signify.

FO: Francis Ouimet (1893–1967) is sometimes called the father of amateur golf in America. He was born in Brookline. The *O* in his initials resembles a golf ball. He is one of only two athletes represented in *The Massachusetts Artifact*.

Spade. The significance of the other details is unknown.

TP: Theodore Parker (1810–1860) was a minister and Transcendentalist. He was born in Lexington.

Row L

Sheet-iron weathervane, according to Duca's notes. It apparently depicts an **angel** blowing a horn.

LF: Lincoln Filene (1865–1957) was a businessman and philanthropist who, with his brother, built his family's business into the iconic Boston department store Filene's. (After a chain bought Filene's, most of its stores became Macy's in 2006. A spinoff company, Filene's Basement, lasted until 2011.) Filene was born in Boston.

Sextant, a maritime navigation device. Duca's notes indicate that this is a tribute to Nathaniel Bowditch (1773–1838). Bowditch was a mathematician whose *Bowditch's American Practical Navigator* was a standard text in the shipping industry for one and a half centuries. He was born in Salem, and lived there and in Boston. The *B* on the plaque probably stands for "Bowditch." Two crescents, one probably representing the moon, appear in the upper left.

ANW: Alfred North Whitehead (1861–1947) was a philosopher who taught at Harvard University.

CRJC: Cardinal Richard J. Cushing (1895–1970) was the Roman Catholic archbishop of Boston and a cardinal, who was widely beloved by people of all faiths. Look for the small *C* above the *R*. (His bust is nearby, at the corner of Cambridge and New Chardon Streets, which is called both Cardinal Cushing Park and Bowdoin Square.)

Bell. It is unknown whether the bell is related to Cardinal Cushing.

Shamrock.

Stencil design.

DANCF: Daniel Chester French (1850–1931) was a sculptor who grew up, lived, and worked in Massachusetts. He created many statues here, including John Harvard and the Minute Man. See pages 25-26 and 83-85.

Row M

HM: Horace Mann (1796–1859) was an advocate for public education and a U.S. congressman. He was born and lived in Massachusetts.

Spring. The source of this symbol and the symbols of the other three seasons is unclear.

Dove of peace.

Seal of the **City of Worcester**. This rendition is only slightly stylized. Worcester's seal does have a heart. This centrally located city calls itself "the heart of the Commonwealth."

FP: Francis Parkman (1823–1893) was a historian and horticulturist. He was born and lived in Massachusetts.

Eagle.

Seal of the **Town of Braintree**. This artifact includes what are apparently miscellaneous design elements unrelated to the seal.

DP: David Porter (1780–1843) commanded several U.S. naval ships, including the USS *Constitution*. He was born in Boston. A star appears above his initials.

Row N

RN: Rebecca Nourse (1621–1692) was convicted of witchcraft during the Salem witchcraft trials and hanged.

Mason's mark for a straight edge.

Owl.

Hebrew letter *tav*. Duca presumably chose this to represent the Jewish presence in and contributions to Massachusetts.

His notes do not indicate why he chose this letter, the last one in the Hebrew alphabet, or if the diamonds and triangle have any significance.

JFK: John F. Kennedy (1917–1963), born in Brookline, was the first president to have poetry read at his inauguration.

WEC: William Ellery Channing (1780–1842) was a Unitarian theologian and minister in Boston. The upper bar of the *E* appears to be part of a cross. (His statue stands in the Public Garden.)

MF: Margaret Fuller (1810–1850) was a reformer, best known as a feminist. She was born in Cambridge.

Rooster.

Winter.

HHR: Henry Hobson Richardson (1838–1886) was the dominant American architect of his time. He lived and worked in Brookline, and designed many buildings in the state.

CDG: Charles Dana Gibson (1867–1944) was an illustrator best known for his pen-and-ink drawings of the Gibson Girl, who was considered the epitome of feminine beauty during the late nineteenth and early twentieth centuries. He was born in Roxbury. An elongated triangle inside the *C* might be a pen.

Row O

JAMcNW: James McNeil Whistler (1834–1903) was a painter who is best known for *Whistler's Mother*. (The painting's formal name is *Arrangement in Grey and Black No. 1*.) He was born in Lowell, Massachusetts.

Bird.

Summer.

Weathervane. This is one of the few things that Duca identified in his notes as an artifact.

Autumn. This piece was cast upside down, Duca noted—but he didn't explain if that was on purpose or, if not, why it couldn't be corrected.

LDB: Louis D. Brandeis (1856–1941) was a U.S. Supreme Court justice who lived and practiced law in Boston before his appointment to the bench.

JWH: Julia Ward Howe (1819–1910) was a social activist, writer, and poet. Her most famous work is "Battle-Hymn of the Republic," whose lyric she set to existing music. She lived in South Boston. (Her bust is in the Boston Public Library. See page 35.)

The significance of this artifact is unknown. It includes the letters "**Ms.**" and **two sunbursts**, one above and a smaller one below. Duca's notes read in their entirety: "Symbol (MS)." Elsewhere in the sculpture, "MS" stands for "Miles Standish," but this is almost certainly not a second reference to Standish. It is unknown whether

Duca intended this as tribute to *Ms.* magazine, which appeared in 1972. It had and still has no special connection to Massachusetts.

Caduceus, a symbol commonly associated with the medical profession.

HWL: Henry Wadsworth Longfellow (1807–1882) was a poet who lived in Cambridge. His most famous poem is "Paul Revere's Ride." (The Longfellow Bridge is named for him. See page 77-78.)

Row P

Potted flower.

GS: Gilbert Stuart (1755–1828) was a painter. His most famous portrait is the one of George Washington that appears on the $1 bill. He lived and worked in Boston.

JSS: John Singer Sargent (1856–1925) was a painter whose portraits and murals are displayed throughout Massachusetts, including at the Museum of Fine Arts, the Gardner Museum, and the Boston Public Library.

WH: Winslow Homer (1836–1910) was a painter and printmaker. He was born and worked in Boston. He lived in Belmont.

Etc.

Ancient **symbol for lime** (the mineral, not the fruit). Duca's notes do not indicate who used this symbol and when, or why he paid tribute to lime, when Massachusetts is not well known for producing it.

JCW: John C. Warren (1778–1856) was a prominent Boston-born surgeon. He was the surgeon during the first public demonstration of ether as surgical anesthesia. William Thomas Green Morton administered the ether; his (erroneous) initials appear in Row J. (A statue and fountain in the Public Garden, called both *The Ether Monument* and *The Good Samaritan*, depicts surgery under anesthesia, but not Warren or Morton.)

SD: Shem Drowne (1683–1774) was a coppersmith, tinsmith, weathervane maker, and creator of the famous grasshopper weathervane on top of Faneuil Hall. He lived and worked in Boston. The flourishes on top of each initial might signify weathervanes.

Row Q

Crescent and Star of Islam.

Seal of the **Town of Newburyport**.

Stencil design.

LH: Learned Hand (1872–1961) was a federal appellate judge in New York. He attended Harvard College and Harvard Law School.

Schooner model.

LHS: Louis H. Sullivan (1856–1924) was an architect who has been called "the father of the skyscraper" and "the father of modernism." He was born in Boston.

Row R

GD: George Dilboy (1896–1918) was born in a Greek settlement in Ottoman Turkey. His family emigrated to Somerville. He fought in the U.S. Army during World War I and died in France.

EAP: Edgar Allan Poe (1809–1849) was a poet, who was born in Boston and had a contentious relationship with the city. (His statue stands in Park Plaza near the Public Garden. See pages 112-115. His bust is in the Boston Public Library. See page 16.)

Pheasant from furniture design.

Asian dragon from a weathervane.

HDT: Henry D. Thoreau (1817–1862) was among other things, an author, poet, naturalist, and leading Transcendentalist. He was born in Concord, and lived and worked in the state.

Printer's symbol, according to Duca's notes.

Seal of the **City of Brockton**.

RWE: Ralph Waldo Emerson (1803–1882) was, among other things, an author, poet, and leading Transcendentalist. He was a friend of Thoreau. He was born in Boston, and lived and worked in Massachusetts.

Row S

NH: Nathaniel Hawthorne (1804–1864) was an author and poet. He was born in Salem, and lived and worked in the state. He was a friend of Thoreau and Emerson.

Lilies.

SC: Samuel Chamberlain (1829–1908) was a soldier, painter, and author. In the Civil War, he was the white commanding officer of the 5th Massachusetts Volunteer Cavalry Regiment, which was all African-American. He grew up in Boston.

Stencil design.

Detail from a tombstone: a **crown inside a heart**.

Row T

Seal of the **Town of Orleans**. Notice the windmill.

Nicola e Bartolomeo: Nicola Sacco (1891–1927) and Bartolomeo Vanzetti (1888–1927)—the *e* between their names is the Italian for *and*—were Italian immigrants and anarchists who were executed for two murders and an armed robbery in Braintree. Their trial, conviction, and execution generated controversy and demonstrations around the world—and are still controversial.

The inclusion of these names caused controversy immediately—even before the sculpture was completed. Two decades after its completion, in 1995, Duca wrote extensively about why he included Sacco and Vanzetti, in more detail than about anything else regarding *The Massachusetts Artifact*. Here are excerpts:

"I am a first generation son of Italian immigrants and a close relative of the now deceased Italo-American newspaper publisher whose offices became the headquarters for the Sacco-Vanzetti legal fund.

"Born in 1920 and brought up in a community of Italo-Americans...it was inevitable that my identity with these two tragic figures would begin to evolve...I still retain a vivid memory of being present at their funeral at age seven, accompanied by my parents and other family members.

"Throughout my life, I have been drawn back to those early childhood experiences.... What in fact remains with me is a not only the questionable 'justice' of their trial, but the sadness to recall that the humble lives of two men, a fish peddler and a cobbler, were terribly destroyed by the machinery of men bent on revenge.

"Thus it was not a capricious act on my part, to engrave the memory of these two men, not as a political statement, but rather as a sincere expression of sympathy for the tragedy and a poignant wish that society would better understand and accept that period in Massachusetts history which brought prejudice and anger to the forefront of people's lives.

....

"After welding, grinding and polishing the entire work, a crew and myself began the tedious task of varnishing it. Starting at the bottom row, we were happily moving along, when whispers of complaints and later, vociferous protests were directed toward us. For I had 'the audacity to place the names of two murderers' in the sculpture. 'Anarchists.'...

....

"[By 1976,] the reaction of the public and the attention given to my inclusion of controversial figures began to overshadow the overall significance of the sculpture. The United Press reported that I had 'memorialized two murderers'...and local Boston media devoted much attention to the issue. I was assaulted daily by passersby while working.

"I had not intended to create a furor, I was simply restating the history of Massachusetts and felt that the integrity of a work of art was being unfairly impugned."

Duca decided: "Instead of polishing and varnishing their plaque, let it be, and allow it to discolor and tarnish over time. I saw this as a fitting symbol of a tarnished moment in history.

"As a result, nearly twenty years later, their plaque is nearly black and the given engraved names 'Nicola and Bartolo' barely visible."

Their plaque is no longer tarnished. Duca himself may have polished and varnished it after May 1995, when he wrote about the controversy. He concluded: "Let those who wish to prolong the debate read and study the voluminous literature concerning the two men and in the process exercise the privilege of being citizens of a free society."

In retrospect, the controversy over the inclusion of Sacco and Vanzetti in *The Massachusetts Artifact* seems incongruous, even quaint. Two years after the sculpture's installation, Governor Michael Dukakis issued a proclamation marking the fiftieth anniversary of the execution, August 23, 1977, as Nicola Sacco and Bartolomeo Vanzetti Memorial Day. The proclamation doubted whether their trial was fair and impartial, and declared that "any stigma and disgrace should be forever removed" from their names. A plaster cast of a memorial plaque to Sacco and Vanzetti is in the Boston Public Library in Copley Square, on the third floor of the McKim building (the older building), near the rare books collection. The John Adams Courthouse, the site of the two highest courts in the state, installed an exhibit to Sacco and Vanzetti in 2007. (As of this writing, the exhibit is still there, years later.)

Meanwhile, Duca's references in *The Massachusetts Artifact* to Daniel Shays, who rebelled against the Massachusetts state government, and to a corrupt felon (see JMSMC on the next page) have apparently generated no controversy.

JLS: John Louis Sullivan (1858–1918) was a boxer who is generally recognized as the first heavyweight champion of gloved boxing. He was born in Roxbury, and was called the "Boston Strong Boy."

Eagle.

Hourglass.

Detail from a **quilting pattern**.

JMSMC: James Michael Curley (1874–1958) served as mayor of Boston for four terms, governor of Massachusetts for one term, and a congressman from Massachusetts for two terms. He also served two terms in prison. Many people consider him to have been a populist champion of the poor and overlook his corruption. (Curley is depicted in not one, but two statues near Quincy Market.)

Row U

SO: Stanislaus Orlemanski (1890–?) was an obscure Roman Catholic priest in Springfield, who, in an obscure incident, flew to Moscow during World War II to confer with Josef Stalin about religious freedom and the fate of Poland.

Cock weathervane.

Stencil design.

At the sculpture's dedication, Duca spoke these words:

"I would dedicate this sculpture, this interval of time, to the people of the Commonwealth of Massachusetts who, from their beginnings, declared for themselves and the nation that freedom is a great possession. I would say that its rhythms, its undulating linear sweep speaks to that quality. I would say that it is the purpose of government to provide a coherent and comprehensive structure in which free choice can be exercised, and that the limits are the limits of the mind to invent new solutions to new problems and that it is the responsibility of its elders in the movement of time to provide some basis of optimism for youth's soaring aspirations. The sculpture represents the inspiration of the artist to express the truest spirit of the Commonwealth, a region of people whose unique intermix of values and energy speak of the fragileness of our purposes and the toughness behind it."

The Massachusetts Artifact commemorates 93 or so people. (An exact count is hard because it is unclear whether the sculpture commemorates Ben Franklin and Nathaniel Bowditch.) A tenth of them—nine people—were poets: Oliver Wendell Holmes (Row B), Emily Dickinson (Row D), E. E. Cummings (Row I), Julia Ward Howe, Henry Wadsworth Longfellow (both Row O), Edgar Allan Poe, Henry David Thoreau, Ralph Waldo Emerson (all Row R), and Nathaniel Hawthorne (Row S).

Poems by some of these nine poets appear elsewhere in the book on the following pages: Dickinson, page 187; Howe, page 36; Longfellow, pages 78 and 81; Poe, pages 116 and 120; and Thoreau, page 20.

Poems by Emerson and Holmes appear below.

Hymn:
Sung at the Completion of the Concord Monument
April 19, 1836
by Ralph Waldo Emerson

By the rude bridge that arched the flood,
  Their flag to April's breeze unfurled,
Here once the embattled farmers stood,
  And fired the shot heard round the world.

The foe long since in silence slept;
  Alike the conqueror silent sleeps;
And Time the ruined bridge has swept
  Down the dark stream which seaward creeps.

On this green bank, by this soft stream,
  We set to-day a votive stone;
That memory may their deed redeem,
  When, like our sires, our sons are gone.

Spirit, that made those heroes dare
  To die, and leave their children free,
Bid Time and Nature gently spare
  The shaft we raise to them and thee.

In 1830, the U.S. Navy announced plans to decommission the USS *Constitution*, nicknamed "Old Ironsides." In response, Holmes wrote a poem "Old Ironsides," which was reprinted and widely read. It helped mobilize public opinion, which changed the Navy's decision. The USS *Constitution* is now the Navy's oldest warship and remains berthed in Boston. The poem "Old Ironsides" is an example of the power of poetry.

Old Ironsides
by Oliver Wendell Holmes

Ay, tear her tattered ensign down!

Long has it waved on high,
And many an eye has danced to see
  That banner in the sky;
Beneath it rung the battle shout,
  And burst the cannon's roar;

The meteor of the ocean air
  Shall sweep the clouds no more.

Her deck, once red with heroes' blood,
  Where knelt the vanquished foe,
When winds were hurrying o'er the flood,
  And waves were white below,
No more shall feel the victor's tread,
  Or know the conquered knee;
The harpies of the shore shall pluck
  The eagle of the sea!

Oh, better that her shattered hulk
  Should sink beneath the wave;
Her thunders shook the mighty deep,
  And there should be her grave;
Nail to the mast her holy flag,
  Set every threadbare sail,
And give her to the god of storms,
  The lightning and the gale!

Questions

Duca honored only those notables who were not alive in 1975, when The Massachusetts Artifact *was installed. Is there anyone, who has died since 1975, whom you think should be honored for his or her contributions or importance to Massachusetts?*

Is there anyone who died before 1975 whom you think should be honored?

What do you think about the reference to Sacco and Vanzetti in The Massachusetts Artifact*?*

What do you think about references to Daniel Shays and James Michael Curley?

If you're continuing to the William Shakespeare bust: It is two stations away on the T, in Chinatown. Go to Park Street Station. (With your back to One Ashburton Place, turn right. Take your first left onto Bowdoin Street. Take your first right onto Beacon Street. Take your first left onto Park Street. The station is at the bottom of Park Street where it intersects Tremont Street.) Take the Red Line toward Braintree or Ashmont; either will do. Get off at the next station, Downtown Crossing. Change to the Orange Line. Take it toward Forest Hills. Get off at the next station, Chinatown. Leave the station, go right on Washington Street, cross Essex Street, and then take your first left onto Beach Street.

If you want to walk (which will take approximately the same time as the T): With your back to One Ashburton Place, turn right. Go left on Bowdoin Street. Go right on Beacon Street. Take your first left onto Park Street. Go right on Tremont Street. Take any of these lefts to Washington Street: Winter Street, Temple Place, West Street, or Boylston Street. Turn right on Washington Street. Turn left onto Beach Street.

WILLIAM SHAKESPEARE

A photograph of this bust appears on the back cover, at the bottom.

Location: 15 Beach Street. Corner of Beach and Knapp Streets.

If you're taking the T: The closest T station is Chinatown on the Orange Line. If you have been riding toward Forest Hills, leave the station, go right on Washington Street, cross Essex Street, and then take your first left onto Beach Street. If you have been riding toward Oak Grove, leave the station, go left, and take your first left onto Beach Street.

If you're driving: Make your way to Chinatown. Find a parking place on the street, in a lot, or in a garage.

What is Shakespeare doing in the middle of Chinatown?

This building was a saloon that was remodeled in 1897 to become the Shakespearian Inn. The bust/plaque of Shakespeare, which is set into the

Title: Unknown
Artist: Unknown
Medium: Cast iron
Date: 1897

facade to the left of the entrance, was presumably installed during the remodeling. Although Washington Street, a block away, is the location of Boston's former theater district and its remnants, Washington Street was not the drama hub in 1897 that it later became. In other words, the presence of the Shakespeare bust is probably not related to how close the theater district used to be.

Here are two sonnets by Shakespeare.

Sonnet 91
by William Shakespeare

Some glory in their birth, some in their skill,
Some in their wealth, some in their body's force,
Some in their garments (though new-fangled ill),
Some in their hawks and hounds, some in their horse,
And every humour hath his adjunct pleasure
Wherein it finds a joy above the rest.
But these particulars are not my measure;
All these I better in one general best.
Thy love is better than high birth to me,
Richer than wealth, prouder than garments' cost,
Of more delight than hawks or horses be'
And having thee, of all men's pride I boast,
    Wretched in this alone: that thou mayst take
    All this away, and me most wretched make.

Sonnet 18
by William Shakespeare

Shall I compare thee to a summer's day?
Thou art more lovely and more temperate.
Rough winds do shake the darling buds of May,
And summer's lease hath all too short a date.
Sometime too hot the eye of heaven shines,
And often is his gold complexion dimmed,
And every fair from fair sometime declines,
By chance, or nature's changing course, untrimmed;
But thy eternal summer shall not fade
Nor lose possession of that fair thou ow'st;
Nor shall death brag thou wander'st in his shade,
When in eternal lines to time thou grow'st;
  So long as men can breathe or eyes can see,
  So long lives this, and this gives life to thee.

For another Shakespeare sonnet, see page 31.

Two blocks away is a site associated with Phillis Wheatley, the poet whose statue is described starting on page 93.

While facing the bust of Shakespeare, go left. At the corner of Beach and Tyler Streets, turn right. Right around and at the corner on Tyler Street is a plaque about Phillis Wheatley.

Location: Tyler Street opposite 2 Tyler Street. Corner of Beach and Tyler Streets. The closest address on Beach Street is 55 Beach Street, which is the building on whose corner the plaque is located.

The plaque reads: "In 1761 at Griffin's Wharf, near this site, John Wheatley purchased eight year old African-American Phillis Wheatley (c. 1753–1784) to serve as a domestic servant. Only twelve years later, in 1773, Phillis Wheatley would become the first published African-American woman with her acclaimed book, *Poems on Various Subjects, Religious and Moral*."

If you're continuing to the Robert Burns statue, it is one station away on the T, Downtown Crossing. Return to the Chinatown Station. Take the Orange Line toward Oak Grove. Get off at Downtown Crossing. Follow the directions after the Robert Burns heading below.

ROBERT BURNS

A photograph of part of this statue appears on the back cover, the upper left photograph.

Location: Winthrop Square.

If you're taking the T: The closest T stations are Downtown Crossing on the Red and Orange Lines, and State Street on the Orange Line.

At Downtown Crossing, look for signs for Washington, Summer, and Winter Streets.

When you leave the station, if you're on a street corner, you're at the intersection of Winter and Summer Streets. Winter Street turns into Summer Street as it crosses Washington Street. Cross the street that you face as you leave the station (Washington Street) and turn right on Summer Street.

When you leave the station, if you're not at a corner, you're already on Summer Street. Turn left.

Walk on Summer Street. Turn left on Otis Street. Otis Street leads to Winthrop Square.

From the State Street Station, leave the station on Devonshire Street and turn right. Devonshire Street leads to and ends in Winthrop Square.

If you're driving: Make your way to Winthrop Square. Find a parking place on the street or in a garage.

> **Title:** *Robert Burns*
> **Artist:** Henry Hudson Kitson
> **Medium:** Bronze and granite
> **Date:** 1919

The Scottish poet Robert Burns (1759–1796) stands on a pedestal that reads simply "Burns," looking downward to viewers and posing with a border collie. In his left hand, he holds a book, with its leaves facing down. In his massive and powerful right hand, he holds a walking stick, which looks as if it were a small limb recently wrenched from a tree. The top of it is jagged and has a twig coming off it. Three acorns in turn are attached to the twig.

Under and behind Burns are thistles, as if he's walking on the heath.

In Scotland, "tartan" means the pattern that Americans call "plaid," and a plaid is a blanket worn across the shoulder. Burns wears a modern plaid (blanket) called a fly plaid, which is not as full as older styles. His plaid is fringed and its tartan pattern is visible on both sides in the cast metal.

A brooch on his left shoulder holds his plaid in place. The plaid falls below his right shoulder, and he grasps it in his right hand. Under his plaid, Burns wears a coat (his left pocket is pulled out) and vest. His stockings are striped.

Burns does not have a particular connection to Boston. Statues to him stand around the world.

In the following poem, *bonie* is *bonnie*, meaning "pretty." *Gang* means "go." *A'* means "all." *Weel* is "well."

A Red, Red Rose
by Robert Burns

O my Luve's like a red, red rose
  That's newly sprung in June;
O my Luve's like the melodie
  That's sweetly played in tune. –
As fair art thou, my bonie lass,
  So deep in luve am I;
And I will luve thee still, my Dear,
  Till a' the seas gang dry. –

Till a' the seas gang dry, my Dear,
  And the rocks melt wi' the sun:
I will luve thee still, my Dear,
  While the sands o' life shall run. –

And fare thee weel, my only Luve!
    And fare thee weel, a while!
And I will come again, my Luve,
    Tho' it were ten thousand mile.

Questions

Is the pedestal too high? Is it hard to view the statue?

Would you prefer that Burns be on your level, as are Edgar Allan Poe (starting on page 112) and the statues in the Boston Women's Memorial 2003 (starting on page 93)?

If you're continuing to Robert Frost's poem "The Gift Outright," walk on Devonshire Street (the Burns statue looks down Devonshire Street) for a few blocks. Enter the Old State House (on the corner of Devonshire and State Streets); the State Street T station is underneath. Take the Orange Line to North Station.

ROBERT FROST'S POEM "THE GIFT OUTRIGHT"

Location: Paul Revere Park, Charlestown neighborhood of Boston.

If you're taking the T: The closest T station is North Station on the Green and Orange Lines.

The 92 and 93 buses, which leave from Haymarket Square, will also take you near the park. After you cross the Charles River, the park will be on your left and the next stop will be the closest. For the 92 bus, the stop will be on Main Street at Park Street. For the 93 bus, the stop will be on Chelsea Street at Warren Street.

If you've taken the T, leave North Station at Causeway Street. Turn right on Causeway Street. The easiest way to walk is to turn left on North Washington Street. (A sign directs you to Charlestown on Route 1 North.) After you cross the bridge, you'll come to stairs on your left. Go down the stairs. Make your way around the playground to the green open oval. You'll see an informal amphitheater space with two long mustard-colored panels set into stone. The panels contain the poem that you're here to read.

If you have taken a bus, make your way to where Chelsea Street intersects North Washington and Rutherford Streets. (North Washington Street turns into Rutherford Street, and vice versa.) Enter the park opposite Chelsea Street. Go down the stairs. When you get to the bottom, you'll be behind a set of stone walls. Go to the other side. You'll see two long mustard-colored panels set into stone. The panels contain the poem that you're here to read.

If you're driving: There is no parking in or next to the park. Look for parking in City Square or on Chelsea Street. Once you've parked, make your way to where Chelsea Street intersects North Washington and Rutherford Streets. Follow the directions in the paragraph above.

In a small lovely out-of-the-way park, set in warm mustard-colored tiles, is a poem by Robert Frost that he read at John F. Kennedy's inauguration in 1961.

The poem is broken into two panels set into low stone bases. The stone bases define the "stage" for a performance space facing a meadow.

I did not secure permission to print "The Gift Outright," but it appears online on many sites.

The poetry installation respects the poem's punctuation and line breaks as it was printed. The top line is hard to read for taller people, who must stoop to read it. Surrounding the poem are tiles depicting leaves, acorns, pumpkins, and other things. (Some tiles are damaged, possibly vandalized by souvenir hunters.) "PRP," which appears on many tiles, stands for "Paul Revere Park." The work of the artist, Susan Gamble, appears throughout the park.

> **Title: None.** The artist avoids titling her work and considers the Robert Frost poem to be part of her larger installation in the park.
> **Artist:** Susan Gamble
> **Medium:** Ceramic
> **Date:** 1999

Paul Revere Park was built in the late 1990s to mitigate the environmental effects of the highway ramps and the Zakim Bridge, which were built over the Charles River. The park was to include public art. The planning director for the Metropolitan District Commission (MDC), which is now the Massachusetts Department of Conservation and Recreation (DCR), and a design consultant were looking for some sort of text to incorporate into the public art. Karl Haglund, Project Manager for the New Charles River Basin for the MDC and later the DCR, suggested Frost's poem. "It's always been one of my favorites," said Haglund (who also authored *Inventing the Charles River*).

A friend of Frost, Stewart Udall, suggested to John F. Kennedy that Frost read a poem at his upcoming inauguration. Udall, a congressman from Arizona, later served as Kennedy's secretary of the interior.

Kennedy telephoned Frost and proposed that he write a poem to mark the inauguration. Frost said no. Kennedy then proposed that he read "The Gift Outright," and suggested changing "would" in the last line to "will," to make it more optimistic and emphatic. This was potentially a sensitive suggestion: that a poet change his work. Accounts differ whether Frost agreed to the change or was non-committal.

Although he initially rejected Kennedy's proposal that he write an inauguration poem, Frost wrote one. He intended to read it as a preface to "The Gift Outright."

At the inauguration on January 20, 1961, Frost, 87 years old, sat for an hour on a very cold day before rising to recite his poetry. Snow, which had fallen the night before, glared off the pages he grasped, and he had trouble reading them. He didn't get through the preface. He stopped and recited from memory "The Gift Outright," which he had completed in 1935. Whatever he had told Kennedy about changing the last line of his poem, he did change it. He read: "Such as she was, such as she would become, has become, and I—and for this occasion let me change that to—what she *will* become."

It was the first time that poetry was recited at a presidential inauguration.

Questions

The poem discusses Americans possessing America. Was the land ours? Or did it belong to other people?

The poem includes this line: "(The deed of gift was many deeds of war)." Was Frost celebrating war as a way to possess land?

Would you ask a poet to change her or his work for a specific occasion? Would you change your poetry for a specific occasion?

Within walking distance, in another park, is a bas-relief silhouette of John Boyle O'Reilly, a poet commemorated by a bronze bust in the Boston Public library and a granite bust on The Fenway. (For information about the bronze bust and one of his poems, see page 35. For information about the granite bust and another two of his poems, see pages 82-86.) The bas-relief silhouette is on a pillar leading into City Square, at an entrance near Park Street. City Square is kitty-corner from Paul Revere Park, across the intersection where North Washington and New Rutherford Streets meet.

If you've walked from North Station, you can return by a different and more picturesque route. Walk to the back of the park. Follow the series of walkways over the water. On your left, you'll be roughly following the bridge that you used to get to the park.

Chapter 4
Davis Square Station, Somerville:
Poetry on the Platforms

Davis Square Station, Somerville: Poetry on the Platforms

─────────── ⌁ ───────────

A photograph of a detail of this installation appears on the back cover, at the top in the center.

When the Davis Square Station on the Red Line opened in 1984, 11 poems were sandblasted into bricks that make up its floor and walkways. The poetry installation was part of the larger Arts on the Line, which brought art to the new stations beyond Harvard Square (Porter Square Station to Alewife Station).

Christopher Jane Corkery, who was involved in the poetry installation, has written that the panel of people charged with bringing art to the Davis Square Station was concerned about "the long expanse of brick flooring on the platforms [and] passageways....The desire to include poetry in the station together with the goal of giving the floor some visual interest led to Poetry on the Platforms." The poems give "people waiting for the train something more than advertisements or directions to read." The art panel considered whether the floor was "the right place for poetry—where it will be stepped on, walked on, looked down on." The answer was a resounding yes, because the panel "liked the immediacy of the floor setting," in contrast to the formality of installing poetry on walls.

A panel of poets and editors picked the poems. Corkery was one. The others were Jonathan Galassi, a poetry editor at Houghton Mifflin, and Lewis Hyde, a poet and translator. Corkery wrote, "Although we wanted some of the poems to be those of well-known American, and preferably New England, poets, we felt that the majority should come from poets now living in Massachusetts. Over 1,500 notices were thus sent to poets throughout the state inviting them to submit poems of nine lines or fewer." Over 400 poets responded.

Corkery and her fellow poetry panelists did not aim to find poems that appealed to everyone. "But we did want to include poems that covered a wide range of interest and talent….The content of the poems ranges from personal to public, serious to humorous, lyric to elegiac. The poets represented are both young and old, famous and unknown, from the country and from the city."

Other details about Poetry on the Platforms are hard to come by—such as whether the bricks were sandblasted before or after they were installed—because decades later, people's memories have faded and documents can't seem to be retrieved.

The poems were "published" in brick, formatted differently than they were published on paper. Indents and line breaks are often different. In addition, the poems were sandblasted in all capital letters. That leads to interesting questions: Is sandblasting poems a form of publication? Do the poems on the platform represent different versions of the poems? And can poems be reformatted without the permission of the poets, some of whom were deceased at the time, even if the poets were being honored by using their work in the installation?

This book records the poems as they are sandblasted, because one never knows if the poems will wear away or be removed in some future renovation. Some of the sandblasted letters are larger than neighboring letters; they represent capital letters, such as at the beginning of sentences; I've reproduced the enlarged letters.

Of the 11 poems in the Davis Square Station, nine are on the train platform. There is no particular order to them on the platform. I'll start with the Walt Whitman poem that is between the inbound and outbound tracks (going to and going from Park Street Station).

If you're taking the T, the Massachusetts Bay Transportation Authority (MBTA), to Davis Square Station and are traveling outbound, the Walt Whitman poem is at the rear of the train. If you're traveling inbound, the poem is at the front of the train.

Two of the poems are outside the station's pedestrian gates. Plan your visit to the station so that you don't have to pay to enter twice. For example, if you have walked to the station and then plan to take the T to Harvard Square, see the two poems outside the gates before entering the station.

Davis Square Station Train Platform

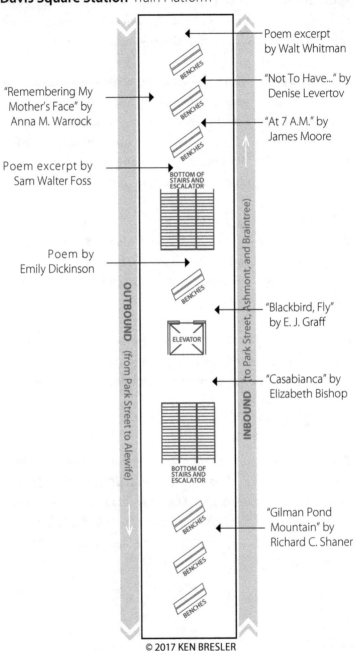

Poem excerpt
by Walt Whitman

"Not To Have…" by
Denise Levertov

"Remembering My
Mother's Face" by
Anna M. Warrock

"At 7 A.M." by
James Moore

BENCHES

BENCHES

BENCHES

Poem excerpt by
Sam Walter Foss

BOTTOM OF
STAIRS AND
ESCALATOR

Poem by
Emily Dickinson

BENCHES

"Blackbird, Fly"
by E. J. Graff

ELEVATOR

"Casabianca" by
Elizabeth Bishop

BOTTOM OF
STAIRS AND
ESCALATOR

OUTBOUND (from Park Street to Alewife)

INBOUND (to Park Street, Ashmont, and Braintree)

"Gilman Pond
Mountain" by
Richard C. Shaner

BENCHES

BENCHES

BENCHES

© 2017 KEN BRESLER

I WILL TAKE AN EGG OUT OF THE ROBIN'S NEST IN
THE ORCHARD,

    I WILL TAKE A BRANCH OF GOOSEBERRIES
    FROM THE OLD BUSH

        IN THE GARDEN, AND GO AND
        PREACH TO THE WORLD;

    YOU SHALL SEE I WILL NOT MEET A SINGLE
    HERETIC OR SCORNER,

YOU SHALL SEE HOW I STUMP CLERGYMEN, AND
CONFOUND THEM,

    YOU SHALL SEE ME SHOWING A SCARLET
    TOMATO,

AND A WHITE

        PEBBLE FROM THE BEACH

           WALT WHITMAN

Unlike most other poems in the installation, this one is not titled. And it's not titled for a reason: It's not a complete poem. This is an excerpt from a poem by Walt Whitman (1819–92). The entire poem follows.

Debris
by Walt Whitman

HE is wisest who has the most caution,
He only wins who goes far enough.

ANY thing is as good as established, when that is
  established that will produce it and continue it.

WHAT General has a good army in himself, has a
  good army;

He happy in himself, or she happy in herself, is
  happy,

But I tell you you cannot be happy by others, any
  more than you can beget or conceive a child by
  others.

HAVE you learned lessons only of those who admired
  you, and were tender with you, and stood aside
  for you?
Have you not learned the great lessons of those who
  rejected you, and braced themselves against you?
  or who treated you with contempt, or disputed
  the passage with you?
Have you had no practice to receive opponents when
  they come?

DESPAIRING cries float ceaselessly toward me, day and
  night,

The sad voice of Death—the call of my nearest
     lover, putting forth, alarmed, uncertain,
This sea I am quickly to sail, come tell me,
Come tell me where I am speeding—tell me my
     destination.

I UNDERSTAND your anguish, but I cannot help you,
I approach, hear, behold—the sad mouth, the look
     out of the eyes, your mute inquiry,
Whither I go from the bed I now recline on, come
     tell me;
Old age, alarmed, uncertain—A young woman's
     voice appealing to me, for comfort,
A young man's voice, *Shall I not escape?*

A THOUSAND perfect men and women appear,
Around each gathers a cluster of friends, and gay
     children and youths, with offerings.

A MASK—a perpetual natural disguiser of herself,
Concealing her face, concealing her form,
Changes and transformations every hour, every mo-
     ment,
Falling upon her even when she sleeps.

ONE sweeps by, attended by an immense train,
All emblematic of peace—not a soldier or menial
     among them.

ONE sweeps by, old, with black eyes, and profuse
     white hair,

He has the simple magnificence of health and
     strength,
His face strikes as with flashes of lightning whoever
     it turns toward.

THREE old men slowly pass, followed by three others,
     and they by three others,
They are beautiful—the one in the middle of each
     group holds his companions by the hand,
As they walk, they give out perfume wherever they
     walk.

WOMEN sit, or move to and fro—some old, some
     young,
The young are beautiful—but the old are more
     beautiful than the young.

WHAT weeping face is that looking from the window?
Why does it stream those sorrowful tears?
Is it for some burial place, vast and dry?
Is it to wet the soil of graves?

I WILL take an egg out of the robin's nest in the
     orchard,
I will take a branch of gooseberries from the old bush
     in the garden, and go and preach to the world;
You shall see I will not meet a single heretic or
     scorner,
You shall see how I stump clergymen, and confound
     them,
You shall see me showing a scarlet tomato, and a
     white pebble from the beach.

BEHAVIOR—fresh, native, copious, each one for him-
    self or herself,
Nature and the Soul expressed—America and free-
    dom expressed—In it the finest art,
In it pride, cleanliness, sympathy, to have their
    chance,
In it physique, intellect, faith—in it just as much as
    to manage an army or a city, or to write a book
    —perhaps more,
The youth, the laboring person, the poor person,
    rivalling all the rest—perhaps outdoing the
    rest,

The effects of the universe no greater than its;
For there is nothing in the whole universe that can
    be more effective than a man's or woman's daily
    behavior can be,
In any position, in any one of These States.

NOT the pilot has charged himself to bring his ship
    into port, though beaten back, and many times
    baffled,
Not the path-finder, penetrating inland, weary and
    long,
By deserts parched, snows chilled, rivers wet, per-
    severes till he reaches his destination,
More than I have charged myself, heeded or un-
    heeded, to compose a free march for These
    States,
To be exhilarating music to them, years, centuries
    hence.

I THOUGHT I was not alone, walking here by the shore,
But the one I thought was with me, as now I walk by
    the shore,
As I lean and look through the glimmering light—
    that one has utterly disappeared,
And those appear that perplex me.

To get to the next poem, "Not to Have…" follow the diagram or these directions: With your back to the Whitman poem, walk straight ahead. The poem is in front of the last bench at this end of the platform, as the bench faces trains arriving on the inbound tracks.

I did not secure permission to print Denise Levertov's poem "Not to Have…" but it appears online on a few sites.

The poem was published in print without indents; with periods at the end of each verse; and with an accent over one *e* in "belovéd."

Levertov (1923–1997) was a major poet who wrote many books of poetry. She taught at Tufts University and other colleges in the Boston area. The Davis Square station is the nearest one to Tufts, but it is unknown whether Levertov's poem was chosen because she taught nearby.

To get to the next poem, "At 7 AM Watching the Cars on the Bridge," follow the diagram or these directions: With your back to the Levertov poem, walk straight ahead.

I did not secure permission to print James Moore's poem "At 7 AM Watching the Cars on the Bridge," but it appears online on various sites.

As originally published, the poem was formatted slightly differently. It had no indents; and had periods after the *A* and *M* in *AM* in the title.

Moore wrote this poem in 1969 or 1970, he told me. The origin of the poem was this sentiment: "I'm a hippie. I'm not going to work. I get to stand on the bridge and be a poet."

At least one reader of the poem has written an online comment assuming that the poem's narrator is suicidal. Moore laughed with surprise when I told him that. "That's what's so great about poetry. You can interpret it so many ways."

Because Moore lives in Minnesota, he wasn't at the dedication ceremony for Poetry on the Platforms. He has been to the station to see his poem only a few times.

Two things particularly delight him about the installation. One is that "you get a whole different audience, not just poetry aficionados." The other is that "it's a permanence that any artist would love." He said facetiously, "Come the final nuclear bomb, I'll have a poem buried deep in the subway system that will survive."

Moore's poem is about not working. The next poem is about working.

To get to the next poem, "Blackbird, Fly," follow the diagram or these directions: While facing the "7 AM" poem, turn right. Walk to the inbound platform edge and go left.

BLACKBIRD, FLY

AS I LEAVE THE SPIT-GRAY FACTORY,
CROWDS OF BLACK BIRDS DRIFT
                UP INTO THE CUMULUS
       LIKE RELEASED BALLOONS.
I HOLD THE WINGS OF MY FINGERTIPS
IN MY COAT POCKET.

E. J. GRAFF

E. J. Graff is a journalist and editor. She wrote "Blackbird, Fly" in her first year after college when she was a temporary worker in a factory. Later, when she was a temp typist, other women who were temps told her about the Arts on the Line project. "All of us temps were artists of some kind," she told me. On the last day of the contest, she submitted this poem. It had not been published elsewhere before being accepted, and it was the first time she had been paid for her writing—a few hundred dollars, she remembers. The format of her poem appears in Davis Square as she wrote it.

Graff suspects that her poem was chosen for the benefit of commuters who were going to work and looking forward to leaving. Because it's a poem about flying that is embedded into an immovable floor, "it's about as contradictory a medium as you can imagine," she said.

To get to the next poem, "Casabianca," follow the diagram or continue walking along the platform.

CASABIANCA

LOVE'S THE BOY STOOD ON THE BURNING DECK
      TRYING TO RECITE "THE BOY STOOD ON
THE BURNING DECK" LOVE'S THE SON
      STOOD STAMMERING ELOCUTION
WHILE THE POORER SHIP IN FLAMES WENT DOWN.

LOVE'S THE OBSTINATE BOY THE SHIP
      EVEN THE SWIMMING SAILORS WHO
WOULD LIKE A SCHOOLROOM PLATFORM,TOO,
      OR AN EXCUSE TO STAY
ON DECK AND LOVE'S THE BURNING BOY

ELIZABETH BISHOP

The poem was published on paper with different indents and more punctuation.

Elizabeth Bishop (1911–1979), was born and died in Massachusetts, and lived in the state and elsewhere. She was the U.S. Poet Laureate from 1949 to 1950 and won the Pulitzer Prize for poetry in 1956.

To get to the next poem, "Gilman Pond Mountain," follow the diagram or continue walking along the platform.

Gilman Pond Mountain

Perched in hackmatack
      and cedar, thrushes
sing and flit, lifting
      Gilman Pond Mountain
up by its hair
      toward morning.

Richard C. Shaner

Shaner wrote the poem with different line breaks and no indents. He is a poet (a not very prolific one, he told me) who lives in Hull. The inspiration for the poem came when he was helping a friend construct a yurt on Gilman Pond Mountain in Maine. They were living in tents, and the thrushes' singing woke them in the mornings. He has also climbed the mountain, which is not tall. The pond is near the peak.

While visiting the station, he has seen people reading his poem. "I have to resist saying, 'Hey, that's mine,'" he said. "I like being next to Elizabeth Bishop and Emily Dickinson."

"Hackmatack," by the way, is a name for a larch tree.

This poem, like "Blackbird, Fly," features birds.

To get to the next poem, follow the diagram or these directions: While facing "Gilman Pond Mountain," turn around. Go past the stairs and escalator. Pass the elevator shaft. Go to the back of the next stairs and escalator.

Emily Dickinson (1830–1886) lived in Amherst. She did not title her poems. A scholar has assigned a number to this one, 260.

I'M NOBODY! WHO ARE YOU?
    ARE YOU - NOBODY - TOO?
THEN THERE'S A PAIR OF US!
DON'T TELL! THEY'D ADVERTISE - YOU KNOW!

    HOW DREARY - TO BE — SOMEBODY!
HOW PUBLIC — LIKE A FROG -
    TO TELL ONE'S NAME - THE LIVELONG JUNE -
TO AN ADMIRING BOG!

EMILY DICKINSON

Dickinson wrote this poem without indents. The capitalizations that she used are not exactly the ones represented by the larger capital letters in the bricks.

To get to the next poem, follow the diagram or these directions: While facing the Dickinson poem, turn left. Walk to the outbound platform and turn right. Pass the elevator shaft. Before you get to the stairs, Foss's poem appears near the edge.

LET ME LIVE IN A HOUSE BY THE SIDE OF THE ROAD
    WHERE THE RACE OF MEN GO BY.
THE MEN WHO ARE GOOD AND
    THE MEN WHO ARE BAD
AS GOOD AND AS BAD AS I
    I WOULD NOT SIT IN THE SCORNER'S SEAT
OR HURL THE CYNICS BANN;
    LET ME LIVE IN A HOUSE BY THE SIDE OF THE ROAD
AND BE A FRIEND TO MAN.

SAM WALTER FOSS

Like the excerpt from the Walt Whitman poem, this selection is not titled. And it, too, is an excerpt from a larger poem.

The poem as sandblasted has "typographical" errors in one line. The word "bann" should have one "n," not two. "Or" should be "Nor." And "cynic's" is missing an apostrophe.

Foss (1858–1911) was a librarian in Somerville. It is of course appropriate that his poetry is in a station in Somerville. This is one of his more famous poems. It appeared in print in 1897. Here's the complete poem.

The House by the Side of the Road
by Sam Walter Foss

"He was a friend to man, and lived in a house by the
side of the road." — Homer.

There are hermit souls that live withdrawn
  In the peace of their self-content;
There are souls, like stars, that dwell apart,
  In a fellowless firmament;
There are pioneer souls that blaze their paths
  Where highways never ran; —
But let me live by the side of the road
  And be a friend to man.

Let me live in a house by the side of the road,
  Where the race of men go by —
The men who are good and the men who are bad,
  As good and as bad as I.
I would not sit in the scorner's seat,
  Nor hurl the cynic's ban; —
Let me live in a house by the side of the road
  And be a friend to man.

I see from my house by the side of the road,
  By the side of the highway of life,
The men who press with the ardor of hope,
  The men who are faint with the strife,
But I turn not away from their smiles and tears —
  Both parts of an infinite plan; —

Let me live in a house by the side of the road
  And be a friend to man.

I know there are brook-gladdened meadows ahead
  And mountains of wearisome height;
That the road passes on through the long afternoon
 And stretches away to the night.
But still I rejoice when the travellers rejoice,
  And weep with the strangers that moan,
Nor live in my house by the side of the road
  Like a man who dwells alone.

Let me live in my house by the side of the road
  Where the race of men go by —
They are good, they are bad, they are weak, they are strong,
  Wise, foolish — so am I.
Then why should I sit in the scorner's seat
  Or hurl the cynic's ban? —
Let me live in my house by the side of the road
  And be a friend to man.

The sandblasted excerpts from Foss's and Whitman's poems have a connection; they both invoke a scorner. It is unknown whether the poetry panel chose the excerpts because of the connection.

To get to the next poem, "Remembering My Mother's Face," follow the diagram or these directions: While facing the Foss poem, continue straight on the outbound platform past the stairs.

REMEMBERING MY MOTHER'S FACE

THE FACE
       IS A JUG OF WATER
DRAWN FROM A WELL
       SMOOTH, SOFT;
THE EYES ARCHED HANDLES
       I LOOK AND LOOK HARD TO HOLD
HER. SHE SMILES — HOW I AM
       THAT SMILE — AND THE WATER
SPILLS

                  ANNA M. WARROCK

Warrock has published two books of poetry, *Turning to Go Back* and *Horizon*. She considers the installation a memorial to her mother, who died when she was a teenager. She lives in nearby Ball Square and has enjoyed seeing people reading her poem in the station. Her poem appeared in print formatted slightly differently.

Despite the name "Poetry on the Platforms," two poems are not on the platforms.

To get to the next poem, "Standing Up," you have to leave the platform. Go up the stairs, escalators, or elevator. Leave the gates and turn left. Go up the stairs, escalator or elevator. When you're on the next level, turn left toward the sign reading "Davis/To Buses." Between the benches and doors leading out are two poems.

Davis Square Station, Ground Level Entrance and Exit, College Avenue

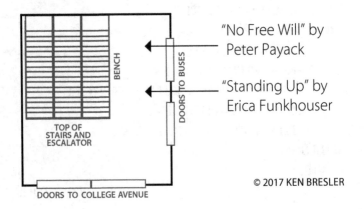

BENCH

DOORS TO BUSES

TOP OF
STAIRS AND
ESCALATOR

"No Free Will" by
Peter Payack

"Standing Up" by
Erica Funkhouser

© 2017 KEN BRESLER

DOORS TO COLLEGE AVENUE

STANDING UP

LIKE A TREE THAT HAS BEEN CHOSEN
     FOR THE OWL'S HOME,
I STAND UP DIFFERENTLY TODAY.

ERICA FUNKHOUSER

This poem is part of a larger poem with a different title.
Funkhouser submitted the excerpt because the call for
submissions specified poems with a maximum of nine
lines. Here is her larger poem.

Waiting

by Erica Funkhouser

i.

I see word of his arrival
in garden cantaloupe:
thread, strand, branch, root.
The veins in the rind
interweave,
do not break.

ii.

Like a tree that has been chosen
for the owl's home,
I stand up differently today.

iii.

New to the sea, he takes
the shape of rivers
that have just left land:
large with freedom
within a larger body.

iv.

Stiller, laden, I hear more
and from darker corners:
the intonations of his shadow,
mine as well.

v.

A painter now, he works all night
on murals, pigments
seeping far into my walls.

vi.
I sink into deep snow
and feel him, restless underlife,
testing his bulk,
tugging as glaciers must
to cut off cliffs.

vii.

If I'm too wide to walk
through these broad valleys,
how will he pass through
a mouth so small
it doesn't even speak?

viii.

He leaves no room for me
to store my old complaints
and secrets. Out every window
they fly – neighbors and strangers
listening.

ix.

He hurries down at last,
his own Niagara –
glistening, no sign
of the interior.

Funkhouser (b. 1949) has published several books of poetry, including *Earthly* and *Pursuit*. A lecturer at the Massachusetts Institute of Technology, she composed a poem for the dedication of the campus memorial to MIT Officer Sean Collier, who was shot on April 18, 2013 by the Boston Marathon bombers.

Thesecondpoemonthestreetlevelisafewstepspastthefirst.

NO FREE WILL IN TOMATOES

I PLACE A TOMATO
ON THE WINDOWSILL
TO RIPEN.

SLOWLY IT TURNS RED.

PETER PAYACK

Payack bills himself as a conceptual anarchist, poet, sky artist, professor, and inventor. The format of Payak's poem, as sandblasted into the bricks, closely resembles how it was published online.

Payack's poem and the excerpt from Whitman's poem have a connection; they both mention a tomato. It is unknown whether the poetry panel chose the poetry because of the connection.

Questions

Do you have a favorite poem in the Davis Square Station?

What do you think about poetry sandblasted into bricks floors in train stations?

With the lighting, how well does this installation work?

The poems are meant to be diverse. Is it incongruous to read about nature, as in "Gilman Pond Mountain," underground in a train station?

Did you see anyone else reading or noticing the poems? Or were most people engaged with their cellphones?

Bibliography
and Sources

Adams, Adeline. *Daniel Chester French: Sculptor.* Boston: Riverside Press, 1932.

The Complete Works of Longfellow. Cambridge: Riverside Press.

Gallo, Joseph R., Jr. *Boston: Bronze & Stone Speak to Us.* Hanover Street Press, 2011.

"An Index to the Persons Commemorated by Inscriptions or Works of Art in the Central Library Building of the Boston Public Library," compiled under the supervision of Frank N. Jones, May 1939 (Boston Public Library reference number: F-A Ref N 521.B6J6).

Meyers, Jeffrey. *Robert Frost: A Biography.* Boston: Houghton Mifflin Co., 1996.

Parini, Jay. *Robert Frost: A Life.* New York: Henry Holt and Co., 1999.

Small, Herbert. *Handbook of the New Public Library in Boston.* Boston: Curtis and Cameron, 1895.

Thompson, Lawrance and Winnick, R. H. *Robert Frost: A Biography.* New York: Holt, Rinehart and Winston, 1981.

Wick, Peter Arms. *A Handbook to the Art and Architecture of the Boston Public Library.* Boston: Associates of the Boston Public Library, 1977.

poetryfoundation.org
poemhunter.com

poetryoutloud.org

famouspoetsandpoems.com

Biographical information in Chapter 3's discussion of *The Massachusetts Artifact* is from Wikipedia.com.

Acknowledgments

Deborah Fogel

Judah Levine

Eve Griffin, Susan Glover,
and the Boston Public Library

Michael Medeiros and the Emily Dickinson Museum

Dana Pilson and Chesterwood

Tonya M. Loveday and the Boston Landmarks Commission

Ronald Hussey and
Houghton Mifflin Harcourt Publishing Company

Joel Leeman, Esq.

Evan Kaplan, Esq.

Richard Duca

Fred Salvucci

Deborah Leipziger

Karl Haglund,
Massachusetts Department of Conservation and Recreation

Laurie Austin, Maryrose Grossman,
and the John F. Kennedy Library

Those who looked at Norbert Wiener's plaque in
The Massachusetts Artifact, page 136: Dr. Howard Smith,
Aviel Klausner, Paul Goldenberg, and Bob Lindenberg

Author

Ken Bresler is a writer and occasional poet who lives in the Boston area. He is the author of *The Witch Trial Trail and the Harvard Witch Walk: The People and Places of Boston and Harvard Connected with the Salem Witch Trials* (Seide Press, 1992); the forthcoming *H. H. Richardson: Three Architectural Tours,* and the editor of *Mark Twain vs. Lawyers, Lawmakers, and Lawbreakers: Humorous Observations* (W.S. Hein, 2014).

CPSIA information can be obtained
at www.ICGtesting.com
Printed in the USA
LVHW050049151220
674148LV00016B/2669